RURAL LONDON
Discover the City's Country Side

First published in Great Britain in 2017 by
Michael O'Mara Books Limited
9 Lion Yard
Tremadoc Road
London SW4 7NQ

A CIP catalogue record for this book is available from the British Library.

Papers used by Michael O'Mara Books Limited are natural, recyclable products made from
wood grown in sustainable forests. The manufacturing processes conform to the environmental
regulations of the country of origin.

ISBN: 978-1-78243-753-6 in paperback print format
ISBN: 978-1-78243-754-3 in ebook format

1 2 3 4 5 6 7 8 9 10

www.mombooks.com

Designed and typeset by Darren Jordan
Cover design by Claire Cater
Cover image © Piero Cruciatti/Alamy

Printed and bound in China

RURAL LONDON
Discover the City's Country Side

KATE HODGES

Michael O'Mara Books Limited

CONTENTS

The path and gateway leading to the walled garden at Osterley Park and House.

INTRODUCTION

London might be the largest urban sprawl in Britain, but that doesn't mean its residents, workers and visitors don't occasionally feel the pull of the land. Whether you're a transplanted country mouse missing your green fix, a born-and-bred Londoner craving peace, or a visitor looking to explore the city's more natural side, you will find something in these pages to inspire you to pull on your boots and get outside.

The longing to get back to the countryside, to reconnect with the natural world, is deep within many of us — even if we live in Zone 1. Choosing to be near world-class art galleries and cutting-edge music venues doesn't render you insensitive to the feeling of grass beneath your toes, the excitement of spotting the orange-and-blue flash of a diving kingfisher or the kick you get from cooking soup using ingredients you've grown yourself. Arm yourself with an emergency list of places to retreat to. Even in

the most concrete of jungles there are hidden arbours, ruined churches covered in moss, nature reserves filled with dragonflies, frogs and rare birds, or atmospheric, misty graveyards, where the noise of the city fades within seconds of stepping in and you can grab a few moments of calm and contemplation.

It may come as a surprise that London is one of the greenest cities in the world. It might not be apparent when you're walking down a smog-choked high road, strolling over concreted squares or watching new developments shoot up, but a survey by Greenspace Information for Greater London has found that an impressive 47 per cent of the capital is verdant land – nearly half of the city is made up of parks, gardens,

The stunning view across London from the Horniman Museum garden.

allotments, conservation sites and much more.

However, it's not always easy to find those rural idylls. City farms with horses, chickens and goats are wedged between railway tracks; little parks full of character are hidden away in urban canyons; and tranquil green oases are concealed behind high walls. By exploring behind the places you see every day or making a trip slightly further afield, you'll be rewarded with peaceful green spaces, secret leafy retreats and people-free walks. Discover London's wild water – where you can paddle in rivers, spot rare birds on reservoirs, or walk through history along a centuries-old canal – then settle down to a pint in a cosy village-style pub that will instantly transport you to the depths of the countryside. Visit windmills, gothic castles, grand country houses and quirky cottages, where you'll find secret walled gardens or unexpected collections of modernist paintings. You'll know some

of these sights well – the big parks and large nature reserves are popular places to visit – but we've teased out the secret corners of the largest spaces and found other, more obscure, treats for you too.

Perhaps you'd like to get more hands-on? Let us help you. Take a foraging or weaving course, learn how to make cheese, volunteer in a community garden, or even take the first steps towards learning how to set up an urban smallholding. Or if you're after something a little more hedonistic, try paddle-boarding, play cricket or learn what the jiggins London skittles is all about. Celebrate change and discover what exciting, multicultural London can bring to British traditions. It's also about discovering the rural pursuits of our neighbours' countries, bonding over weeding an overgrown border in the street and creating communities dedicated to improving the shared environment.

This book is not about escaping London. Rather, it's about rediscovering another side to the city, a side that's always been here, hanging on by its feral claws among the luxury apartments and work/play piazzas. It's about catching a little respite from the rat race while staying within the M25 and getting some peace without having to take a two-hour train trip. It's about finding beauty in a place that might seem unforgiving and harsh, about building relationships in a place that might seem unwelcoming, about finding solace in tradition and about wondering at the resilience of nature and its primal, restorative powers.

WOODLAND

According to Greenspace Information for Greater London, there are eight million trees in London, which makes the city the world's largest urban forest. The villages that went on to make up the sprawl of the city used to be swathed in woods. Examples of ancient forests include the Great North Wood, which stretched from Deptford to Streatham and down to Selhurst; the Forest of Middlesex, which ran twenty miles (32 km) north of the city walls and covered much of what is now north London; and Hanging Wood in Charlton, which was a notorious spot for highwaymen.

There are still plenty of fragments of ancient woodland left, perfect for exploring, building dens in, dog walking and climbing trees. There are also more modern wooded areas, created on reclaimed patches of land or from old Victorian gardens. Woods have a special atmosphere of their own; visit on a damp autumn morning to search for mushrooms, go in the summer to snatch precious shade, or tramp through them in winter, all boggy leaf mulch and piney scents. The traffic noise recedes fastest of all when you enter a wood, a simple way to slip away from the strains of city life.

The dense, atmospheric woodland of Epping Forest.

EPPING FOREST
Take time to discover your favourite spot

Epping Forest can seem daunting: it's huge and on a hot summer's day it can seem like the whole of Essex is determined to get some shade. The blockbuster haunts are the visitor centres: the View, Queen Elizabeth's Hunting Lodge and the Temple – avoid them if you want some space to yourself. For peace, head to the forest's secret spots: the views of the city's smoggy spires from Yates' Meadow and Pole Hill; the sand and gravel left from the Ice Age found at High Beach; and birdspotting nirvana at Higham's Park, part of the forest's Special Area of Conservation. Visit Eagle Pond for wildfowl, including flotillas of swans, and Hollow Ponds for a refined row. One of the most peaceful ways to explore the forest is on horseback and there are riding centres across the area. It's London's largest open space – there are 131 square miles or 339 square kilometres of forest to explore, so take it slowly.

cityoflondon.gov.uk/things-to-do/green-spaces/epping-forest/ ♀ *The Warren, Loughton, Essex, IG10 4RW* **FREE** *24 hours* *Epping, Theydon Bois, Debden Roydon overground* *There is wheelchair access*

RUSSIA DOCK WOODLAND
Uncover this area's maritime past

Formerly one of the Surrey Commercial Docks, here you'll still find old bollards, chains and tracks dotted about this long, narrow spur of green land, now a peaceful oasis in a busy part of London. Spot herons and kingfishers in the series of ponds, wander along a trail through the trees or explore the wood's many interesting nooks and crannies. Children will love the natural play area and a post-runaround climb to the top of Stave Hill to see the panoramic view is a must-do.

southwark.gov.uk/info/461/a_to_z_of_parks/664/russia_dock_woodland ♀Redriff Road, SE16. **FREE** ⏲24 hours 🚊Canada Water ♿There is wheelchair access

COLDFALL WOOD
Uncover prehistoric secrets

A wild space set behind the manicured, semi-detached houses of Muswell Hill, Coldfall Wood is small but a pleasure to explore. In 1835 excavations here found marine fossils, shells and rocks from the north of England, which proved to historians that glaciers once covered most of England and the Welsh mountains – a monumental discovery now half-forgotten. Oaks and hornbeams have replaced those icy beasts and now make up the majority of trees in this sylvan paradise, much loved by dog walkers and children. Explore the marshy stream, picnic on the wide-open meadow and enjoy the great children's play area.

🖉 *haringey.gov.uk/libraries-sport-and-leisure/parks-and-open-spaces/z-parks-and-open-spaces/coldfall-wood* 📍 *Creighton Avenue, N10 1NT* **FREE** 🕐 *24 hours* 🚌 *Finchley Central* ♿ *There is wheelchair access*

THE TOTTERIDGE YEW
Living history in wood form

The oldest living thing in London isn't to be found in the zoo, or even in a fancy park. In deepest, darkest (actually incredibly rural-feeling) Totteridge, there's a tree that in 2008 was declared to be about 2,000 years old – almost as old as the city itself. The Totteridge Yew has a girth of over 7.5 metres (25 ft) and was once the meeting point for a medieval justice gathering, the Hundred Courts. Visit today and get the thrill of being able to touch a real piece of history, as well as the opportunity to wander around a graveyard that feels as if it should serve a country parish.

🖉 *totteridgechurch.org.uk* 📍 *44 Totteridge Village, N20 8PR* **FREE** 🕐 *24 hours* 🚌 *Totteridge and Whetstone* ♿ *There is wheelchair access*

SYDENHAM HILL WOOD
Hunt the curiosities within

The mix of ancient woodland (it's the largest bit still left of the old Great North Wood), modern trees and Victorian garden plants and ornaments make this a distinguished place for a wander. Walk down avenues shaded by foliage on both sides, discover a monkey-puzzle tree and find the disused railway tunnel, dark and forbidding. Come in spring and early summer to forage for wild garlic and take pictures of the bluebells.

wildlondon.org.uk/reserves/sydenham-hill-wood-and-coxs-walk ♀*Crescent Wood Road, SE26 6LS* **FREE** *24 hours* *Sydenham Hill overground* *There is wheelchair access*

QUEEN'S WOOD
A remnant of old England

Tangled with huge ancient trees, this space has been continuously wooded since at least 1600 and was originally part of the Forest of Middlesex. It's wilder than neighbouring Highgate Wood, with oaks and beeches spreading out above hazels and hollies. Come here near Christmas to gather festive branches or in spring to take in the restorative powers of the carpet of wood anemones. It's full of nature – spot owls and bats, or frogs in the little pond. It's a popular place with dog-walkers, but never feels crowded – even in the height of summer it's easy to lose yourself and find a quiet space to dream. Have a sit in one of the supersized branch dens towards the Wood Vale end and conclude your visit with a cup of organic soup from the community-run cafe.

haringey.gov.uk/libraries-sport-and-leisure/parks-and-open-spaces/z-parks-and-open-spaces/queens-wood-local-nature-reserve ♀ Muswell Hill Road, N10
FREE ⏱ 24 hours 🚇 Highgate ♿ There is wheelchair access

TOWER HAMLETS CEMETERY PARK
Hunt toads among the tombstones

Created as one of the 'Magnificent Seven' London cemeteries built for a growing metropolis, Tower Hamlets Cemetery was closed to burials in 1966 and became a designated park. Not only are there gloriously gothic tombstones to explore and elaborate carvings to uncover, it's also home to a thriving nature reserve. Most of the reserve is woodland, but there's a smattering of meadows and wildlife ponds teeming with frogs, butterflies, birds, newts and bees. There are regular events held at the park, including a Saturday morning kids' wildlife club, a forest school with outdoor activities and guided walks, which put it at the heart of the community, with a real focus on nature. For a truly immersive experience, download their 'Meet Me at the Cemetery Gates' sound walk.

🖱 *fothcp.org* ♥ *Southern Grove, E3 4PX* **FREE** ⏲ *24 hours* 🚊 *Mile End, Bow Road* ♿ *There is wheelchair access*

BARNSBURY WOOD
Wildlife reclaims a garden for its own

Originally the garden of a vicarage, Barnsbury Wood is now the smallest nature reserve in London and home to long-tailed tits, lesser stag beetles, common toads and sixteen-spot ladybirds. Enter this titchy triangular copse through tall iron gates and you'll feel like you've stepped into a hidden garden from a Victorian gothic novel. However, the buzz of the Caledonian Road is only a few minutes' walk away. It's only open for a few hours each month – savour every minute.

🖱 *islington.gov.uk/sports-parks-and-trees/nature-reserves/barnsbury-wood* ♥ *Crescent Street, off Huntingdon Street, N1 1BT* **FREE** ⏲ *Tuesdays 2 p.m.–4 p.m., Saturdays 2 p.m.–4 p.m. (July–September)* 🚊 *Caledonian Road* ♿ *There is wheelchair access*

GARDENS

Every one of the capital's gardens is different. Some are private and usually inaccessible to curious eyes: most Londoners have peeped over railings into the private squares of Kensington, or wondered what's going on behind the high walls of Buckingham Palace. However, not all gardens are out of bounds. There are secret, formal arbours hidden in the depths of parks or tucked behind museums. Some even teach visitors about rare plants, the social history of outdoor spaces or medicinal and useful botanicals. Not all gardens are stiff and formal: we've included some that are newly built, determinedly modern and used as venues for art shows, performances or workshops. Some are perfect for a little breather and a sit-down on a bench surrounded by fragrant blooms, while others are huge and will fill days and days with pleasure. Return to your favourites in different seasons and be rewarded: from the first peeping of the snowdrops to the stark and dramatic bare branches of winter, even the same place gives new and unexpected treats as the year turns.

One of the majestic peacocks at the Kyoto Garden.

HORNIMAN MUSEUM AND GARDENS
Floral curiosities inspired by the museum's quirky collections

With views across the city and fresh air on tap, these gardens are an eccentric place to spend a leisurely couple of hours. There's an animal walk with goats and llamas, and a half-mile, wild-feeling nature trail that winds along the site of an old railway line. Much of the garden takes inspiration from the bizarre and hugely varied objects found in the museum. The formal flowerbeds of the dye garden contain marigolds, dahlias and other plants used to colour fabric. There's also a medicinal garden filled with herbs and natural remedies, a sweet-smelling rockery and a twenty-foot-high totem pole peering out onto London Road.

---

horniman.ac.uk 100 London Road, SE23 3PQ
FREE Museum open daily 10.30 a.m.–5.30 p.m.;
Gardens open 7.15 a.m.–sunset Forest Hill
There is wheelchair access

BREAKER'S YARD
As hip as its east London location

Once derelict scrubland, Breaker's Yard adjoins Sutton House, a picturesque sixteenth-century building with oak panelling and carved fireplaces. This small Shangri-la, formerly a car breakers' yard, is a quirky garden that fits perfectly into Hackney's hip environs. Twist around the carefully constructed paths to find a 1970s caravan that's been transformed into a stately home, a painted ice-cream van and gates covered in toy cars donated by celebrities. Both garden and house host creative events such as immersive theatre, children's workshops and off-the-wall film nights. Thoroughly modern, but still a retreat from the urban world.

---

nationaltrust.org.uk/sutton-house-and-breakers-yard
2 and 4 Homerton High St, E9 6JQ **FREE** Breaker's
Yard £Sutton House Wednesday–Sunday 12
p.m.–5 p.m.; open daily in August, bank holiday
Mondays and Good Friday Hackney Central
Ground floor of house only

ROYAL BOTANIC GARDENS, KEW
London's pinnacle of botanic achievement

The grandaddy of gardens, Kew is a jaw-dropping example of show-stopping flora, rare-beyond-belief plants and a world-class horticultural science hub. It contains over 30,000 different kinds of living plants in its 300 acres, which are scattered with wonderfully eccentric glasshouses and other structures. It's gigantic (the gardens even have their own police force) and, while there are must-sees such as the Nash Conservatory and Pagoda, there are tucked-away sights that might pass beneath your radar. Meander in the velvet-lawned Duke's Garden, hidden behind high walls and scented with lavender. Find the Waterlily House, where dark ponds are crowded with leaves like green flan dishes and delicate flowers. In early summer, the Rose Pergola is a magical place to wander through, garlanded heavily with fragrant blooms. The gardens reward repeat viewings, being as spectacular in the snow as in the warm sun. It's tempting to become a Friend of Kew so you can visit as often as you like and benefit from two extra visiting hours in the summer.

kew.org ♀ Richmond, Surrey, TW9 3AB £ ⊙ Gates open at 10 a.m. all year round. Closing times vary according to season, so check online first 🚇 Kew Gardens
♿ There is wheelchair access

GEFFRYE MUSEUM GARDENS
Travel through horticultural time

Plonked incongruously on the takeaway-crammed, traffic-heavy Kingsland Road is a serene block of almshouses transformed into a museum of interiors, with rooms decorated in the style of different periods. Reflecting those rooms are the Geffrye's period gardens, each of which represents a century from the seventeenth onwards. There are knot gardens, shrubberies, pools and beds, all of which will teach you something about the city's past, as well as being pleasant places for a wander. If it's a rainy day, scoop up a design book from the comprehensive collection in the reading room and take it to the conservatory at the back of the building. Sit on a cane chair looking out over the beautiful scene and lose yourself in words and pictures.

geffrye-museum.org.uk 136 Kingsland Road, E2 8EA **FREE** Tuesday–Sunday 10 a.m.–5 p.m.; closed Mondays, except bank holiday Mondays 10 a.m.–5 p.m. Hoxton, Old Street There is wheelchair access

HAM HOUSE
Graceful grounds surround the stateliest of homes

Most of the gardens here are as formal as black-tie-and-tails, with sharp-edged box hedges and a cherry garden filled with plump, round lavender cushions. The kitchen garden is bursting with produce – enough to provide the cafe with fruit and vegetables all year round. Head to the Wilderness to explore the summer houses, play hide-and-seek or have a picnic. Take the nearby Hammerton's Ferry across the River Thames from the north bank for an adventurous approach to the house.

nationaltrust.org.uk/ham-house-and-garden
♀Ham Street, Ham, TW10 7RS £ ⓘHouse 12 p.m.–4 p.m. 1 January–4 March and 10 October–31 December: selected rooms open, by guided tour at certain times. Garden 10 a.m.–5 p.m. Cafe, garden and shop close at dusk if earlier than 5 p.m. 🚇Richmond ♿There is wheelchair access

CHRISTCHURCH GREYFRIARS
A floral elegy to a lost church

Designed by Sir Christopher Wren and built between 1687 and 1704, Christchurch Greyfriars was destroyed by fire in the Second World War, leaving only the west tower. In 2011 the grounds were transformed and turned into gardens. Blue, white and purple roses climb around wooden trellises and towers, built to replicate the original church towers and pews. A short hop from St Paul's Cathedral, right in the heart of the city, this is a sliver of rural tranquillity.

*cityoflondon.gov.uk/things-to-do/green-spaces/ city-gardens/visitor-information/Pages/christchurch-greyfriars-church-garden.aspx ♀King Edward Street, EC1 **FREE** ⓘ24 hours 🚇St Paul's ♿There is wheelchair access*

BONNINGTON SQUARE GARDEN
Co-operative living in the city

Bonnington Square was reborn in the 1980s, when squatters formed a housing co-operative and created a volunteer-run cafe and community garden on a bombed-out section of the area. It's now been renamed The Pleasure Garden, and is an oasis of leafy calm in a busy area. Make sure to look out for the 9-metre iron waterwheel left over from the Industrial Revolution. On the square is the wonderful vegetarian and vegan-orientated Bonnington Cafe, a community-run, very affordable restaurant with a collective of cooks, where you can eat Italian, French or Japanese food by candlelight. Bring your own bottle of wine and sway home dreaming of communal, utopian living.

bonningtonsquaregarden.org.uk ♀Bonnington Square, SW8 1TE **FREE** *Dawn to dusk (if it's locked, then the local delicatassen, Italo, has keys); cafe open seven days a week 12–2 p.m., 6.30–10.30 p.m. Vauxhall There is wheelchair access*

OLD ENGLISH GARDEN, BATTERSEA PARK
Breathe in the scents of England

Once neglected and sad, the Old English Garden was given a makeover in 2015 by designer Sarah Price, funded by delicious-scent manufacturer Jo Malone. The garden is now a stunning place to visit and, of course, smells divine. The restoration came courtesy of the Thrive project, which uses gardening to change the lives of disabled people. The garden's previously formal edge has been blurred, with plants spilling over from the beds and onto the paths. It's a bucolic place, filled with evocative scents, but has a modern feel.

batterseapark.org/nature/gardens/old-english-garden/ ♀SW11 4NJ **FREE** *6.30 a.m.–10.30 p.m. Battersea Park and Queenstown Road overground There is wheelchair access*

CHELSEA PHYSIC GARDEN
Working plants hard since 1673

The oldest botanical garden in London, with over 5,000 edible, useful, medicinal and historical plants, Chelsea Physic Garden is a plant nerd's heaven. Wander around the informatively presented beds, smelling eucalyptus leaves, pomegranates and grapefruits. The garden is divided into sections and we especially like the Woodland Garden, a shaded place to find out about practical and therapeutic plants from forest environments around the world. The Tangerine Dream Cafe serves home-baked cakes and locally sourced food – take an out-of-town friend for afternoon tea with lavender scones. Visit in spring to catch the garden's wonderful collection of snowdrops, or at Christmas for an atmospheric fair, full of gift ideas inspired by nature.

chelseaphysicgarden.co.uk 66 Royal Hospital Rd, SW3 4HS £ Tangerine Dream Cafe, garden and shop open Tuesdays–Fridays and Sundays 11a.m.–6 p.m. Garden only is open on Mondays 10 a.m.–5 p.m. Sloane Square There is wheelchair access

KYOTO GARDEN
A tiny, exquisite taste of Japan

Like many of the best things to come out of Japan, the Kyoto Garden is small but perfectly formed. Situated in Holland Park and donated in 1991 by Kyoto's Chamber of Commerce, it was conceived as a place for quiet contemplation. If you hanker after that tranquillity, it's best to come early in the morning to avoid the crowds. Wander around its carefully designed waterfalls, spot koi in the ornamental ponds and snap an Instagram-friendly peacock. Secret nooks and crannies abound in this incredibly central park. Visit the orangery, enjoy the formal beds that come alive with perfect blooms and walk in acres of wilder woodland.

rbkc.gov.uk/leisure-and-culture/parks/holland-park ♀*Holland Park Ave, W11 4UA* **FREE** *7.30 a.m.– half an hour before dusk* *Notting Hill, High St Kensington* *There is wheelchair access*

RED CROSS GARDEN
Volunteer or simply enjoy

Created by philanthropist and co-founder of the
National Trust Octavia Hill in 1887, Red Cross
Garden was an 'open-air sitting room' and a living
demonstration of the importance of good housing
and meaningful employment for the poor plus contact
with nature for overcrowded city residents. The original
layout was designed for leisure and beauty, with
fountains, a bandstand, mosaics and a covered play
area, which a 2005 restoration of the place aimed
to echo. It's a well-kept, inspiring place to visit, with
dramatic views of the Shard, some very cute little
almshouses to admire, and places to sit and enjoy a
quiet moment. If you're lacking in garden space and
have itchy green fingers, it's a great place to volunteer.

---

bost.org.uk/open-places/red-cross-garden/ ♀*50
Redcross Way, SE1 1HA* **FREE** *9 a.m.–5 p.m.
Closed Sundays London Bridge, Borough There
is wheelchair access*

BUILDINGS

From rose-rambled cottages to windmills, London is studded with buildings that seem to have been transplanted from the four corners of the United Kingdom. In reality, many of these places are fragments from when London was a string of villages and hamlets – little pockets of the city untouched by bombs, developers or hipsters.

Steal a summer afternoon to visit a rustic building for an escape to cooler air, or take a retreat in winter. All the places mentioned in this chapter are open to the public at least some of the time, to satisfy those with a penchant for peeking behind closed doors. Once inside, you might find a collection of paintings, wonderful views of the city, a folk music concert or one of the best tea rooms in town.

Looking up towards Kenwood House.

BRIXTON WINDMILL
Get flour powered on an urban estate

Brixton is full of extraordinary sights, but perhaps the most surreal of all is the 200-year-old working mill tucked behind a modest housing estate just off Brixton Hill. Set in immaculately cared-for community gardens, the mill produces stoneground flour and is the hub for a series of events that include bat walks, milling demonstrations and a harvest festival. Book ahead for a full tour of the building, where you'll climb into the upper chambers to see the wind-powered machinery, or take the shorter, drop-in peek at the first level only. Don't leave without buying a packet of their flour.

brixtonwindmill.org ♀*West end of Blenheim Gardens, off Brixton Hill, SW2 5EU* **FREE** *Book tickets ahead.* ⊕*Open selected weekends through the spring and summer* 🚇*Brixton* ♿*Very restricted*

ST PANCRAS OLD CHURCH
Wander through central London's village churchyard

A leafy sanctuary hidden just behind St Pancras Station, the Old Church is a piece of ancient London that's somehow managed to survive into the twenty-first century. It looks like a country chapel, with a square tower topped with a jaunty roof and is surrounded by a grassy, cleared graveyard dotted with a few mausoleums. Don't miss the Hardy Tree, an ash that's been encircled by layers of tombstones purported to have been arranged by the poet Thomas Hardy who, around 1865, was employed to clear space in the churchyard to make way for the new Midland Railway line. Take time out to sit in the shade, while listening to the Eurostar trains on the other side of the perimeter wall and imagining their exotic destinations.

posp.co.uk ♀*Pancras Rd, NW1 1UL* **FREE** ⊕*Check website for service times* 🚇*King's Cross* ♿*There is wheelchair access*

OSTERLEY PARK AND HOUSE
Enjoy country grandeur and luxurious gardens

Osterley is one of the last surviving country estates in London. This 'palace of palaces' is an imposing red-brick mansion with an interior encrusted by gilt-framed paintings, elaborate ceilings and ornate carving, all in French chocolate-box shades of duck-egg, crimson and pink. It's the kind of place you'd usually drive miles into the countryside to visit, yet it's just off the A4 between Hammersmith and Hounslow. Revel in the gorgeous gardens and acres of landscaped parkland, too.

nationaltrust.org.uk/osterley-park-and-house ♥ *Jersey Rd, Isleworth, TW7 4RB* £ *House open 11 a.m.–5 p.m.; gardens open 10 a.m.–5 p.m.* *Osterley* *Wheelchair access to ground and principal floors*

KENWOOD
Take tea at this neoclassical super-villa

Standing at the top end of Hampstead Heath, the denizens of NW3 and NW5 treat the clotted-cream-coloured mansion of Kenwood as the most beautiful of social hubs. In summer, it's the place to eat sorbet while watching impromptu cricket matches on the gentle slopes that stretch towards a picturesque pond. In winter, it's a wonderful, sheltered place to meet friends and take in the extraordinary collection of paintings, then drink strong coffee and nibble lemon-scented cakes in the cafe.

english-heritage.org.uk/visit/places/kenwood/ ♀*Hampstead Lane, NW3 7JR* **FREE** *House open 10 a.m.–4 p.m.* *Highgate* *Level access throughout ground floor. Easy staircase with continuous handrail to upper floor*

ST DUNSTAN-IN-THE-EAST
Find solace amongst the concrete in this former church

A pocket of green sandwiched between buildings and a hop from the Tower of London, St Dunstan-in-the-East is a stop-off point for those in need of a quick chlorophyll fix. Damaged in 1666 by the Great Fire of London, patched up, then bombed during the Second World War, the remains of this Anglican church now make an eerily beautiful place for contemplation, with palms and winter's bark twining around the ruins.

cityoflondon.gov.uk/things-to-do/green-spaces/city-gardens/visitor-information/ Pages/St-Dunstan-in-the-East.aspx ♥*St Dunstan in the East, St Dunstan's Hill, EC3R 5DD* **FREE** ⏱*Open from 8 a.m.–7 p.m. or dusk, whichever is earlier* 🚇*Tower Hill* ♿*There is wheelchair access*

VALENTINES MANSION
Find contemporary art in an idyllic setting

Built at the tail end of the seventeenth century, Valentines Mansion in Ilford is a (fairly) newly restored secret retreat, complete with kitchen gardens, a dovecote and rococo grottos. Wander around the Victorian kitchen and Georgian rooms, or enjoy one of their seasonal events (their Christmases are always special). The place isn't some ossified mausoleum, however: venture upstairs and there are a series of contemporary artists' studios, very much used and loved – visit them on one of their regular open studio days. Leave time in your trip for lunch at the Gardener's Cottage Cafe, situated in the walled garden and a dreamy place to eat on a warm summer's day.

---

valentinesmansion.com ♥*Emerson Road, Ilford, IG1 4XA* **FREE** *⏰Open Tuesdays 11 a.m.–3 p.m., Sundays 11 a.m.–3 p.m. During the school holidays, the venue is also open Mondays and Wednesdays 11 a.m.–3 p.m* 🚇*Gants Hill* ♿*Width restrictions for larger wheelchairs*

SEVERNDROOG CASTLE
Revel in gothic splendour just off the South Circular

With a name that could be straight out of a Mervyn Peake novel, Severndroog Castle is a dramatic, fairy-tale tower that looks as if it should be jutting proudly from the edge of a windswept Yorkshire cliff. Instead, it stands just a short hop from the South Circular Road, in the ancient tangles of Oxleas Wood on Shooter's Hill. Climb to the top for dramatic, leaf-framed views of the neat suburbs of Kidbrooke, the tower blocks of Woolwich and, rising in the distant smog, the City's skyscrapers. Then descend to the wood-panelled Castlewood Tea Room for a slice of homemade cake and a milkshake.

---

severndroogcastle.org.uk ♥*Castle Wood, Shooters Hill, SE18 3RT* **£** *⏰Open Thursday, Friday and Sunday: spring/summer 12.30 p.m.–4.30 p.m.; autumn/winter 11 a.m.–3 p.m.* 🚇*Eltham overground* ♿*Limited to ground floor via a stair climber (notify the venue in advance on 0800 689 1796)*

SOUTHSIDE HOUSE
A house full of extraordinary objects and stories

Gloriously eccentric, Southside House is a world away from a stuffy stately home. Decorated in a mishmash of historical styles, it is stuffed with things old and not-so-old that have piqued the interests of the owners over the years. The house feels genuinely soaked in history – it's a little ramshackle, which only gives the place more atmosphere – and the tales of the Pennington Mellor Munthe families who have owned it are like something from a *Boy's Own* adventure story. The gardens feel like those of a country house: perfect for playing hide-and-seek.

southsidehouse.com ♀3–4 Woodhayes Rd, Wimbledon Common, SW19 4RJ £ ⊕Open Easter Sunday–late September on Wednesday, Saturday, Sunday afternoons and Bank Holidays ☐Wimbledon overground &No access for wheelchairs and walking frames

FENTON HOUSE
Uncover refined pleasures and treasures in this modest stately home

National Trust property Fenton House is a genteel seventeenth-century house on the fringes of Hampstead Heath, without the bustle of nearby Kenwood. Take in the paintings, marvel at the views across London from the balcony and browse the collections of early musical instruments while listening to soothing live music. If you want to feel like you're truly in the country, however, the enchanting walled garden is the place in which to stroll. Lose yourself in neat box hedges, fragrant herbs and the bountiful orchard. An hour spent here can feel like a weekend in a quiet country house.

nationaltrust.org.uk/fenton-house-and-garden ♀Hampstead Grove, NW3 6SP £ ⊕House open 11 a.m.–5 p.m.; garden open 10 a.m.–5 p.m. ☐Hampstead &Ground floor only: two steps to entrance, ramp available. Grounds partly accessible

PARKS

London is a city built around parks and Londoners' lives revolve around them. With many of us having tiny gardens, balconies or no outside space at all, they're where we live our outdoor lives. These green spaces are where we party on our birthdays, learn to ride our bikes, drunkenly play cricket, run through at dawn every morning or kiss at sunset.

Some of our parks are grand: the eight Royal Parks (Bushy Park, The Green Park, Greenwich Park, Hyde Park, Kensington Gardens, The Regent's Park, Richmond Park and St James's Park) are the big hitters, all sweeping lawns and powerhouse attractions. But even they have secret, hidden treasures, some of which we've included in this chapter.

Then there are the smaller, everyday parks and recreation grounds, where we take our children to scoot and that we doggedly jog around after Christmas. We've found some that punch above their weight and go beyond the traditional lawn-and-flower-bed format to bring a touch of the country to urban lives.

You'll also discover some little parks that have survived against the development odds or that have been carved from unpromising ground. These green spaces are like pause buttons that we should all help to preserve: places to stop for a short while and regroup.

London's parks are our everyday link to the countryside that surrounds the city.

One of the historic bridges over the River Wandle at Morden Hall Park.

BLACKHEATH COMMON
Wild winds and big skies

Blackheath feels like a prairie, stretching flatly from the top edge of Greenwich Park to Blackheath village in the south. It has a sinister past – all plague pits, highwaymen and peasants' revolts – a real-life *Horrible Histories* setting. Nowadays, the open space is perfect for flying kites, feeling the bluster of a windy day or for running in the elements and its vastness makes it perfect for a party. It's a place where south London comes together: fireworks and bonfires on Guy Fawkes night, music festivals in the summer and funfairs in spring.

blackheath.org SE3 **FREE** 24 hours Blackheath *There is wheelchair access*

RICHMOND PARK
A park fit for a king

This vast, beautiful area is the biggest enclosed space in London. Rolling across the south-west of the city, it is home to herds of magnificent deer and big enough to lose yourself in. Walk up to King Henry's Mound for spectacular views towards St Paul's Cathedral or, on a rainy day, have a cup of tea in the elegant Pembroke Lodge tearooms. The Isabella Plantation, a woodland garden filled with Technicolor blooms, is our favourite spot. It's forty-two acres rich with flowers and is famous for azaleas, rhododendrons and camellias, at their psychedelic peak in late April and early May. Sit by one of the many streams or ponds and revel in immersive natural artworks. Children love to play on the stepping stones and watch the ducklings learning to swim. Arrive early to avoid the crowds and bring a picnic.

royalparks.org.uk/parks/richmond-park ♀Holly Lodge, TW10 5HS **FREE** ⊕Vehicle access: summer 7 a.m.–dusk, winter 7.30 a.m.–dusk. Pedestrian access 24 hours a day, except during deer cull in November and February, 7.30 a.m.–8 p.m. ⊒Richmond (District line and overground) ♿There is wheelchair access

MORDEN HALL PARK
A beautiful, community-focused park

The River Wandle threads through Morden Hall Park's 125 acres of greenery, which is peppered with preserved watermills, cottages, farm buildings and the spectacular-but-sadly-empty Morden Hall itself. The rose garden is particularly beautiful, with thirty-eight flowerbeds filled with different varieties. It's a great place to bring children: there are meadows in which to run, wetlands to explore and its National Trust status means there are always plenty of activities, from crafts inspired by nature to den building and even overnight camp-outs. Adults pack the free, guided history walks that run on Sundays between March and November. This cleverly used park provides a chance to get up-close to the natural world, while retaining a strong sense of history.

---

nationaltrust.org.uk/morden-hall-park ♀Morden Hall Rd, SM4 5JD FREE ⊙Rose garden open 8 a.m.– 6 p.m. in summer, 8 a.m.–5 p.m. in winter ♿Grounds partly accessible with loose gravel paths

HAMPSTEAD HEATH
Rugged and bucolic but only a hop from the centre of town

The gigantic Hampstead Heath is only four miles (6 km) from Trafalgar Square, but wild enough to ramble across and daydream of Yorkshire moors. It's hugely popular, but there's plenty of space in which to lose yourself in. Our favourite, lesser-known spot is Cohen's Fields, the meadows set at the top of the heath, next to Kenwood. It's a lovely place to picnic, with views across the London skyline. At the north end of the heath are Hill Gardens and the Pergola, a raised, column-lined walkway, crumbling with grandeur and twined in vines. Come on a misty morning in autumn when the ruins are truly, surreally beautiful.

---

cityoflondon.gov.uk/things-to-do/green-spaces/ hampstead-heath ♀NW3 FREE ⊙24 hours ⊞Hampstead, Belsize Park, Kentish Town, Hampstead Heath, Gospel Oak overground ♿There is wheelchair access

POSTMAN'S PARK
Read tales of heroism in this pocket oasis

Shaded by skyscrapers and glass buildings, this patch of green space is a miniature lung for the city. Weekday lunchtimes, you'll rub shoulders with office workers eating their sandwiches, but, off-peak, this park is either sun-dappled heaven or deliciously gloomy. Most interesting are the plaques commemorating the heroism of everyday people: read miniature Victorian melodramas of those who lost their lives rescuing fellow humans from fires, railway lines and rivers – the kind of inscriptions you'd expect to find in a dusty country church.

🖱*cityoflondon.gov.uk/things-to-do/green-spaces/city-gardens/visitor-information/Pages/Postman's-Park.aspx* 📍*Postman's Park, St Martin's Le Grand, EC1A* **FREE** 🕐*Open 8 a.m.–7 p.m. or dusk, whichever is earlier* 🚇*St Paul's* ♿*There is wheelchair access*

TRENT COUNTRY PARK
Rural life at the end of the Piccadilly line

Just a ten-minute walk from Cockfosters underground station, Trent Country Park feels like you've stepped into the English countryside. You might see a combine harvester baling up neat parcels of hay, a buzzard circling lazily overhead or a muntjac deer careering off into the forest. It's a place full of treasures: woods to explore, playgrounds to burn off energy (including the hugely popular Go Ape) and the quirky Animal Centre, residence of rescued deer, ducks, rabbits and guinea pigs and home to a playground and some of the most peculiar taxidermy known to man.

🖱*trentcountrypark.com/Welcome.html* 📍*Cockfosters Rd, EN4 0PS* **FREE** *Park* £*Animal Centre* 🕐*Monday–Saturday from 8 a.m., Sundays from 8.30 a.m. Closing times vary* 🚇*Cockfosters, Oakwood* ♿*There is wheelchair access*

GREENWICH PARK
Elegant city panoramas and naval history

Perhaps the most majestic of all the London parks, the bottom of Greenwich Park is ringed with Georgian houses, bow-windowed and elegant, rather like a smart country-market town. The top of the hill commands astonishing, green-leaves-meet-skyscrapers views towards the City and across to the centre of town. Head to the statue of General Wolfe at sunset to see the skyline at its most breathtaking. Want wildlife? Explore the Wilderness, where woodlands with ancient trees provide a sanctuary for a herd of red and fallow deer, foxes, stag beetles and mice.

royalparks.org.uk/parks/greenwich-park SE10 8QY **FREE** 6 a.m.–various, depending on the season Blackheath, Greenwich and Maze Hill overground There is wheelchair access

WATERLOW PARK
Find culture in Highgate's green playground

Poised genteelly near the top of Highgate Hill,
Waterlow Park's position lifts it out of the smog and
into near-bracing territory. It boasts three ponds
filled by natural springs, exotic flower beds and wide,
open slopes, but the real jewel is Lauderdale House.
This sixteenth-century building is a hub for the local
community, hosting art classes for kids and adults,
a beloved Christmas grotto and outdoor theatre
performances, often held amid the stone sculptures on
the terrace as the sun sets, soaked in atmosphere.

waterlowpark.org.uk *Highgate Hill, N6 5HG*
FREE *7.30 a.m.–various, depending on the season*
Highgate, Archway *There is wheelchair access*

WIMBLEDON COMMON
Womble around this suburban wilderness

Wimbledon Common is huge and wild-feeling;
when Putney Heath and the Lower Common are
taken into consideration, it covers 1,140 acres. It's
heathland rather than a formal park; explore the
hidden-away Queensmere Pond, nature reserves
Farm Bog, Fishponds Wood and Beverley Meads, or
the remnants of an Iron Age hill fort. Despite the
picnicking families there's a rugged feel to the place,
the trees are higgledy-piggledy and paths are winding.
The Wimbledon Windmill is an unexpected sight – step
inside to find a museum dedicated to flour grinding.

wpcc.org.uk *SW19* **FREE** *Open 24 hours*
There is wheelchair access

SPRINGFIELD PARK
East London's unsung riverside idyll

BECKENHAM PLACE PARK
A place that slowly reveals its secrets

With areas of ancient woodland, meadows, a rose garden and a run-down, Scooby Doo-style 'country' house, this park is full of quirky places to explore. Come in the spring to see it carpeted with bluebells, or in high summer to enjoy the butterflies flitting around flower-filled meadows. The park is a listed nature reserve, so take your bird-spotting guide and a pair of binoculars. The Visitor Centre is situated in the eighteenth-century mansion – go in to grab a leaflet or two and have a poke around its beautiful rooms.

A sorely underrated park, Springfield is where the red-brick housing blocks and phone shops of north-east London start to fragment and melt into the countryside. Here you'll find a cricket pitch, tennis courts and fountains, as well as wonderful views out east across Walthamstow Marshes and beyond into Essex. There's also a cook-from-scratch cafe, housed in the grade II-listed White Lodge Mansion. The park is at its loveliest at the foot of the hill, where the River Lea runs by. Spot parakeets, kingfishers and terrapins and watch barges cruise along the river. It's not just like being in the country: in this context, it feels like being in a different country.

*beckenhamplaceparkfriends.org.uk ♀Beckenham Hill Rd, SE6 3AG **FREE** ⊙9 a.m.–5 p.m., closed Sundays 🚆Beckenham Junction, New Beckenham and Lower Sydenham overground ♿There is wheelchair access*

*hackney.gov.uk/springfield-park ♀Springfield Mansion, E5 9EF **FREE** ⊙Open 24 hours. Opening hours of sports facilities vary according to season – check online in advance 🚆Clapton overground ♿There is wheelchair access*

BROCKWELL PARK
Swim, ride a tiny train or help out in the greenhouses

Filled with interesting things to do, Brockwell Park is an easy place to spend a whole day. The gorgeous art deco lido is a cool place to hang out on hot days and invigorating on winter mornings. There's a miniature railway for small kids to ride on and a BMX track for bigger ones. Climb the hill to visit the early nineteenth century Brockwell Hall, which houses a cafe. The former kitchen garden of the house is now a walled rose garden – don't miss the chance to drift through the flowers. In the centre of the park, the Brockwell Park Community Greenhouses (brockwellgreenhouses. org.uk) host free family gardening, baking and crafting workshops, which are the stuff of legend among the south-London mums' community.

🖱 brockwellpark.com 📍 Norwood Road, SE24 9BJ
FREE 🕐 7.30 a.m.–15 minutes before sunset
🚇 Herne Hill overground ♿ There is wheelchair access

ALEXANDRA PALACE PARK
Climb the hill for rewarding views across the north of London

Alexandra Palace dominates the north-London skyline, sentinel over Crouch End. The park it's set in is sloped and lush; head high for fresh air and views right across to sister radio mast Crystal Palace in south London. The park feels at its most rural at its base: pick past the pitch and putt course, down to the cricket pitch, where there may well be a match you can sit and watch from the boundary line. Then on to the marshy ponds at the eastern side, where there are bullrushes, frogs and blackbirds and, if you're very lucky, a pair of peregrine falcons.

🖱 alexandrapalace.com/park/ 📍 Alexandra Palace Way, N22 7AY **FREE** 🕐 24 hours 🚇 Alexandra Palace overground ♿ There is wheelchair access

SECRET
SANCTUARIES

When the grime and chaos of the city get too much to bear, it's good to have a place to which you can retreat. You might regain your equilibrium with an outdoor lunch in a shady spot, take a Sunday morning walk to breathe in some fresh air under wide skies, or spend an evening watching the sunset, surrounded by flowers and with a drink in your hand. Green oases are hidden in the most unlikely places in the city: tucked behind tower blocks, wedged in behind cinemas and West End theatres and even on top of familiar buildings.

Some are more exotic: conservatories filled with palms, Japanese-style gardens, or places that transport you to countryside spots in the far corners of the globe. There are also concealed corners of popular parks; find secret, walled gardens, pockets of lavender or romantic, flower-bedecked nooks in which to steal a kiss or two. We've gathered some of our favourite spots here.

The spectacular Kensington Roof Gardens are a real escape from the city.

QUEEN ELIZABETH HALL ROOF GARDEN
A green plot with spectacular views

Sit among sunflowers, fruit trees and wildflowers while drinking in a view of Big Ben, the London Eye and St Paul's (and drinking in some refreshments from the bar, too). This mini patch of greenery sits on top of the concrete brutalism of the Southbank Centre, its green leaves and gentle petals nuzzling the harsh (but rather beautiful) edges of the 1960s building. There are often bees buzzing around the blooms courtesy of the hives on top of the Royal Festival Hall. It's a lovely place to come for a post-work, evening wind-down, or to have a drink before watching a concert at the Royal Festival Hall. There are often workshops and classes taking place on the green lawns – take your kids to learn to make clay pots, or try your hand at writing poetry inspired by the unusual view.

---

southbankcentre.co.uk/venues/Queen-Elizabeth-Hall-Roof-Garden ♀Belvedere Road, SE1 8XX **FREE**
Open in spring and summer, 10 a.m.–10 p.m.
Embankment, Waterloo &There is wheelchair access

HYDE PARK PET CEMETERY
A surreally sad burial ground

Created in 1881 by a gatekeeper at Victoria Lodge
who started burying people's pet dogs in the garden,
the Hyde Park Pet Cemetery is an odd little place
that most Londoners are unaware of. It's not easy
to get into – either contact Royal Parks for a private
visit, or wait for a rare public tour. Once in, however,
it's a curious little slice of history. The pets belonged
mainly to rich owners who lived in the graceful streets
surrounding the park, their passing marked by heart-
rending inscriptions on minuscule gravestones: 'Darling
Dolly, My Sunbeam, My Consolation' reads one. This
place feels like a true refuge from the real world.

---

*supporttheroyalparks.org/events ♀Bayswater Road,
SW7 1NR £ ⊕By appointment ☒Lancaster Gate
⬅There is wheelchair access*

BARBICAN CONSERVATORY
Green fronds soften hard concrete lines

Wedged deep in the brutalist concrete of the Barbican
Centre is a glass-covered oasis of greenery. Open
to the public most Sundays and bank holidays, this
palm-and-cactus-filled sanctuary is both chlorophyll-
saturated and warm and dry. Take a break from the
maze of unforgiving walkways and never-ending floors
of the centre and spot a terrapin or the odd bird, or
let your mind drift as you watch the koi carp float
aimlessly around the pond.

---

*barbican.org.uk/visitor-information/conservatory
♀Level 3, The Barbican, Silk St, EC2Y 8DS **FREE**
⊕Most Sundays and bank holidays (check online)
☒Barbican ⬅ Limited access for wheelchair users
and people with restricted mobility due to steps in
some areas*

THE ROOKERY
A mosaic of gardens at the top of the hill

NUNHEAD CEMETERY
Acres of ivied graves to explore

With spectacular, unexpected views towards the city (the glimpse of St Paul's Cathedral through a peephole in the trees will make you catch your breath), Nunhead Cemetery is a bucolic-feeling spot that restores and inspires. Walk up a tree-lined avenue to the ruined chapel, picturesque and gothic and with sightlines back towards the London Eye. Take a winding route through the fifty-two acres, listening for the hammer of woodpeckers and watching for jays. The monument of John Allen is spectacular – look for stone lions guarding an arched memorial – and the Scottish Martyrs monument and Dissenters Road add a sharp tang of rebellion to the place.

Set at the top of the hill on Streatham Common, The Rookery is a secret maze of neat, formal gardens, flower-garlanded arbors, pagodas and ponds. Leave the sunbathers, dog-walkers and football players of the common behind and lose yourself in a sweet-smelling labyrinth of fountains, sundials and waterfalls with stepping stones. It's a wonderful place to explore – take delight in turning corners to uncover new treasures and romantic nooks – then sit on one of the many benches to take in the pretty vistas. Part of the old nursery area of the site is now a community garden, which aims to preserve the historic features and become a growing hub for people from all walks of life from Lambeth.

fonc.org.uk *Linden Grove, SE15 3LP* **FREE** *8.30 a.m.–varies according to season* *Nunhead overground* *There is wheelchair access*

lambeth.gov.uk/places/the-rookery *Covington Way, SW16 3BX* **FREE** *7.30 a.m.–15 minutes before sunset* *Streatham Overground* *There is wheelchair access*

ST JOHN'S LODGE GARDENS
Concealed elegance and tranquillity

Push open a blink-and-you'll-miss-it gate on the Inner Circle of Regent's Park to find this hidden treasure. Built to be a garden 'fit for meditation' in 1889, it's a peaceful haven-within-a-haven; the nymph statues, trailing wisteria flowers, green arches and stone bowers spilling with blooms provide respite from the heady(ish) clatter of the park's bandstands, ice-cream vans and zoo. Spot butterflies in the summer and crunch on frosted paths in the winter. It's peaceful, very English and one of the best-kept secrets in central London.

royalparks.org.uk/parks/the-regents-park/things-to-see-and-do/gardens-and-landscapes/st.-johns-lodge-gardens ♀ Inner Circle, NW1 4NX **FREE** 🕐 5 a.m.–dusk 🚌 Regent's Park, Great Portland Street, Camden Town ♿ There is wheelchair access

EEL PIE ISLAND
A bohemian hideaway with a touch of rock 'n' roll

Long beloved of artists and musicians (The Rolling Stones, The Who and Black Sabbath all played legendary shows at the Eel Pie Island Hotel, which used to stand on the site), Eel Pie Island is now home to a nature reserve, a few higgledy-piggledy houses and twenty-six artists, whose studios are clustered around a working boatyard. The place is only accessible via footbridge from the north bank or boat, but is fully open twice a year during the summer for open-studio weekends. The awkwardness of getting to it is also its saving grace – it feels undeveloped, a little ramshackle and a true retreat for creatives, which makes it a rare treasure in this part of the world. There are abandoned sculptures, rusted iron gates and houses painted in unexpected pinks and blues. Take the opportunity to take in some stunning art and have a good look around this cloistered-by-the-river community.

eelpieislandartists.co.uk ♀ *Twickenham, TW1 3DY* **FREE** *Open studio weekends every summer* 🚇*Twickenham overground* ♿*Access by footbridge only. Some studios inaccessible for wheelchair users*

HIGHGATE CEMETERY
Revel in Gothic splendour

The most well known of all the London burial grounds, Highgate is dramatic, grand and very gothic. The setting for numerous Hammer horror films, it's the final resting place of many famous people, including Douglas Adams, George Eliot, Malcolm McLaren and Lucian Freud. The tombs are on a grand scale – big monoliths, fragile, winged angels and the imposing Circle of Lebanon, which is half Egyptian, half classical. Roam the East Cemetery at your leisure – it's where Karl Marx is buried – or book a guided tour of the Victorian west side. It's easy to lose yourself in the east side – even on a hot summer's day there are plenty of shady nooks to explore and the peaceful, leafy atmosphere is calming and restorative.

---

highgatecemetery.org *Swain's Lane, N6 6PJ* £ *East side: March–October weekdays 10 a.m.–5 p.m., weekends 11 a.m.–5 p.m.; November – February open until 4 p.m. West side: weekdays book in advance only, weekends 11 a.m.–4 p.m.* *Archway* *There is wheelchair access*

KENSINGTON ROOF GARDENS
A green wonderland in the sky

Make an upwards flight from the flash-car-filled, pearls-and-leather streets of Kensington to a real English country garden. Opened in 1938 atop a beautiful art-deco building, the gardens consist of three different areas: the Spanish Garden, the Tudor Garden and English Woodland, plus an elegant bar. The English Woodland will transport you to a fragrant, leafy place: visit in the spring to catch the snowdrops, bluebells and crocus flowers. You may even make the surreal sighting of one of the tame flamingos roaming about the place. Check ahead that the gardens are open on the day you choose to visit and be sure to take photo ID with you.

roofgardens.virgin.com ♀*99 Kensington High Street, W8 5SA* **FREE** ☺*Call for opening times (sometimes closed for events): 0207 937 7994* 🚌*High Street Kensington* ♿*There is wheelchair access*

ABNEY PARK CEMETERY
Find peace among the crumbling tombstones

Step off bustling Stoke Newington High Street into Abney Park Cemetery and within thirty seconds you'll be in shady heaven. The grave of Salvation Army founder William Booth and his wife, Catherine, is one of the first you'll see, but wander in deeper and you'll find little tombstones, square memorials and, our favourite, a life-sized lion that commemorates menagerist Frank Bostock. Track round paths towards the centre of the graveyard and you'll find the oldest surviving (just – it is sadly derelict) non-denominational chapel in Europe, designed to lack bias towards any one Christian sect. The park is well used by man and nature – you'll rub shoulders with dog-walkers, joggers, woodpeckers and owls, but its winding nature means it's easy to find your own, secluded space.

abneypark.org ♀*Stoke Newington High St, N16 OLH* **FREE** *8 a.m.–dusk* *Stoke Newington overground* *There is wheelchair access*

BUNHILL FIELDS BURIAL GROUND
Drink in radical history and literary legends

The non-conformist nature of this graveyard contrasts sharply with the ultra-conservative financial district it abuts. Home to the graves of John Bunyan, Daniel Defoe and William Blake, this scrubby patch of green is a retreat right at the very heart of the most urban part of London. In the spring, crocuses bloom across the lawns and in summer you may even spot a pair of jays or spotted flycatchers flitting from tomb to tomb. Poet John Milton lived on Bunhill Row, on the west side of the cemetery, until his death in 1664. Take a breather from the traffic, noise and relentless grind of the city, sit under a typical London plane tree and immerse yourself in *Paradise Lost*.

cityoflondon.gov.uk/things-to-do/green-spaces/city-gardens/visitor-information/Pages/Bunhill-Fields.aspx ♀*38 City Road, EC1Y 2BG* **FREE** *8 a.m.–7 p.m. or dusk, whichever is earlier* *Old Street* *There is wheelchair access*

WILDLIFE AND NATURE RESERVES

The development of London continues at a desperate rate, but there are some refuges for wildlife proving to be immune so far from burial in concrete. There are 144 declared nature reserves in the city, home to foxes, hedgehogs, kingfishers, woodpeckers and water voles. In them, you'll find wild flowers, meadows, wooded areas and swampy wetlands. Some of the reserves are pocket-sized with just enough space for wildlife to catch its breath and survive, fitted in behind train tracks, under flyovers or behind homes. Others are enormous, running down entire waterways or old railway lines, or spreading out luxuriously next to the Thames. All of them contribute to Londoners' well-being, either spiritually, by providing a place to commune with nature; educationally – many of them run workshops and classes for adults and children; or community-wise, as most are powered by volunteers. There's no better way to engage with both the land and your fellow man than working alongside your neighbours and friends to improve green spaces in your 'hood.

Greenwich Peninsula Ecology Park is home to beautiful flora and fauna.

WOODBERRY WETLANDS
State-of-the-art facilities at the newest reserve in town

Opened by David Attenborough in 2016, these forty-two acres of ponds and swampy ground contrast sharply with the tower blocks of the nearby Woodberry Down estate. The two former reservoirs at the heart of the reserve were saved by local residents, who use the west water for sailing, kayaking and swimming. Owned and managed by the London Wildlife Trust, the ultra-modern facilities and walkways sit comfortably with the flora and fauna. Birds are the superstars here — see visiting ospreys, swifts, swallows, buzzards and red kites. Plus, of course, the resident ducks, geese, kestrels, sparrowhawks and warblers. The reserve hosts a series of varied events from woodworking and foraging days to bat walks and foraging rambles and is a place for jaded city residents to commune with nature. Don't leave without trying fresh coffee and home-made cake at friendly Lizzy's at the Coalhouse cafe.

---

woodberrywetlands.org.uk ♀*West & Coal House entrance: New River Path via Lordship Road, N16 5HQ; East & New River Studio entrance: 1 Newnton Close, N4 2RH* **FREE**
9 a.m.–4.30 p.m. *Manor House, Stamford Hill overground* *There is wheelchair access*

CAMLEY STREET NATURAL PARK
Bird-watching and pond-dipping round the back of the Eurostar terminal

Hewn in 1984 from an old coal yard at the back of King's Cross station, this creatively designed oasis is a deep-green jewel in the centre of one of the most built-up areas of town. Wander through a mini-woodland, past the quirky cafe (their cakes are out of this world), past a series of ponds and onto Viewpoint, a floating platform inspired by tiny Finnish islands. Situated on the Regent's Canal, it's a wonderful spot to have a packed lunch, spot birds and dragonflies and watch the world go by on the towpath opposite. The reserve is also a great place to bring kids for a breather during a busy day out in the centre of town and there are often pond-dipping sessions or nature workshops going on at weekends and in the holidays.

🖋 *wildlondon.org.uk/reserves/camley-street-natural-park* 📍*12 Camley Street, N1C 4PW* **FREE**
🕐 *Winter 10 a.m.–4 p.m.; summer 10 a.m.–5 p.m.*
🚇*King's Cross* ♿ *There is wheelchair access*

LONDON WILDLIFE AND WETLAND CENTRE
Spot rare migrant birds and rare migrant present deliverers

One of the big hitters of London nature reserves, the London Wildlife and Wetland Centre is only a short flit from Hammersmith, yet feels like you're in the heart of the countryside. Created from four disused Victorian reservoirs near the Thames in Barnes, it consists of 100 acres of lakes, ponds and gardens. This is a blockbuster day out, especially for families; alongside the hides, paths, otters and voles, there are adventure playgrounds, giant tunnels, the Discovery Centre (which uses games to explore water-based habitats around the world) and a pool with an underwater camera. Around Christmas you might even find reindeer, huskies or Father Christmas in his grotto.

🖋 *wwt.org.uk/wetland-centres/london/* 📍*Queen Elizabeth's Walk, SW13 9WT* £ 🕐*Winter 9.30 a.m.–4.30 p.m.; summer 9.30 a.m.–5.30 p.m.* 🚇*Barnes Bridge overground* ♿ *There is wheelchair access*

RAILWAY FIELDS
Take time out to learn about London's wildlife

Cleverly planted to screen off the smog and rattle of nearby Green Lanes, the 2-acre Railway Fields has education at its heart, but is also a rewarding place to spend a little time with nature. Formerly a railway goods yard, it's now home to a teaching building used for environmentally themed classes. Explore the reserve to find wild flowers, including the unique Haringey Knotweed, a cross between Japanese Knotweed and Russian Vine. Although it's small, twenty-one kinds of butterfly and over sixty species of bird have been recorded here.

---

*tcv.org.uk/railwayfields ♀381 Green Lanes, N4 1ES **FREE** Monday–Friday 9 a.m.–5 p.m., plus last Saturday of each month and alternate Sundays Haringey Green Lanes overground There is wheelchair access*

GUNNERSBURY TRIANGLE
A hard-won slice of flora and fauna

Formed between railway tracks behind Chiswick Park underground, this three-sided piece of wild land feels truly hidden away. It's a lovely place for a tranquil wander, with paths winding through wooded areas, a pond, marsh and meadow, and is home to woodpeckers, sparrow hawks, newts, frogs and toads. Appropriately for a reserve fought for and won by people power (and still having to continue fighting development in the area), it holds regular, community-focused events such as fungus-hunting forays and family days with pond-dipping and crafts.

---

*wildlondon.org.uk/reserves/gunnersbury-triangle ♀Bollo Lane, W4 5LW **FREE** 24 hours Chiswick Park There is wheelchair access*

GREENWICH PENINSULA ECOLOGY PARK

Lakes and the Thames form this watery sanctuary

Almost within coughing distance of the Blackwall Tunnel, the Ecology Park provides 27 acres of chloro-filled goodness. There's a couple of ponds, a small woodland area, a lush meadow perfect for summer picnics and a couple of hides for winter birdwatching. We're fans of their events; the Winter Fair is a green rather than red-and-white way to celebrate the festive season, with wreath-making and quiz trails.

tcv.org.uk/greenwichpeninsula ♥ *John Harrison Way, SE10 0QZ* **FREE** *Wednesday – Sunday: spring–summer 10 a.m.–5 p.m., autumn–winter 10 a.m.–dusk* *North Greenwich* *There is wheelchair access*

WILDERNESS ISLAND
Fall into two arms of the River Wandle

Created from the remnants of seventeenth-century mill works and a Victorian pleasure garden (an ornamental fish pond is still in place), Wilderness Island is living, breathing proof that nature will always claw back its territory. Follow the nature walk between two arms of the River Wandle (it's part of the trail – see page 129), and spy on woodpeckers, grebes, butterflies, kingfishers and the grey wagtails that breed in the weir. Visit in the early spring to enjoy organized pond-dipping sessions and see gelatinous frogspawn, baby newts and water boatmen skimming across the surface of the water.

wildlondon.org.uk/reserves/wilderness-island
Mill Lane, Hackbridge, SM5 2NH **FREE** *Open 24 hours Hackbridge rail station No wheelchair access. There are public footpaths but the terrain is difficult in places*

GILLESPIE PARK
Watch out for flying footballs

Squidged behind Arsenal underground station and almost in the shadow of the Emirates Stadium, this is Islington's biggest nature reserve. It's a green lifeline for the local community; there are ponds, woodlands and meadows and an Ecology Centre, which holds great little events and gives advice on wildlife, gardening and sustainable living. Once discovered, it's the kind of place you'll return to again and again for nature spotting, relaxation and an escape from the harsh, urban environment.

islington.gov.uk/sports-parks-and-trees/nature-reserves/gillespie-park-and-ecology-centre ♀*191 Drayton Park, N5 1PH* **FREE** *8 a.m.–dusk. Closed when events take place in Arsenal Stadium. Ecology Centre open Monday to Friday 10 a.m.–4 p.m., weekend opening varies.* *Arsenal, Finsbury Park* *There is wheelchair access*

PEREGRINES AT TATE MODERN
Front-row seats for the feathered Grand Prix

Birds of prey are breathtaking creatures: their hooked beaks, huge wings and lightning speeds (up to 200 mph or 322 kph) make them the celebrities of the bird world. Peregrine falcons nearly became extinct in the 1960s, but their numbers have recovered astonishingly, so that there are now thought to be thirty nesting pairs in London. Every summer, RSPB volunteers man telescopes on the south side of the river, near the Millennium Bridge, to give great views of the birds found swooping around the Tate Modern. It's a close encounter with wildlife, a reminder that we share our space with impressive beasts and a spectacular way to encounter birds right in the heart of the city.

rspb.org.uk ♀*Millennium Bridge, Bankside, SE1 9TG* **FREE** *11 a.m.–6 p.m.* *Mansion House, St Paul's* *There is wheelchair access*

LEE VALLEY PARK
Explore the many wildlife habitats on offer

The Lee Valley Park is a huge 'green lung' that runs across the east of London, from the Thames, right up to Ware in Hertfordshire, following the route of the River Lea. It's vast and takes in campsites, woods, farm parks, reservoirs, canals and nature reserves. Our favourite spots include WaterWorks Centre and Middlesex Filter Beds (E10) with their huge bird hide, kingfishers and newts; Three Mills Island's (E3) towering tidal mill and eco-playground; Tottenham Marshes (N17), where you might see kestrels or rare bee orchids; and Walthamstow Marshes (E10), home to rare plants, water voles and grazing cattle.

leevalleypark.org.uk **FREE** ⏲24 hours
🚇Tottenham Hale ♿There is wheelchair access

CRANE PARK ISLAND
Uncover London's explosive past while enjoying nature

On the site of the old Hounslow Gunpowder Mills, Crane Park Island is a dreamily beautiful, woody place. If you're quiet and very lucky, you'll spot diving kingfishers and water voles splashing in the River Crane. There are still bits of mill machinery lurking in the undergrowth and the nineteenth-century Shot Tower is now home to the visitors' centre, which holds excellent art classes for kids and workshops for adults.

wildlondon.org.uk/reserves/crane-park-island
📍Ellerman Avenue, TW2 6AA **FREE** ⏲24 hours. The Shot Tower is open on Sundays 1.30 p.m.–4.30 p.m. and for special events 🚇Whitton overground ♿Shot Tower accessible at ground floor only

STAVE HILL
Get a bird's-eye view of the city

Created from scratch, Stave Hill Ecological Park is just over the river from Canary Wharf – head up adjacent, man-made Stave Hill for stunning views across to Docklands and the City. The park welcomes volunteers, running regular sessions every Wednesday (10 a.m.–4 p.m.) and on the second Saturday of each month (11 a.m.–3.30 p.m.). These are highly rewarding ways to get back to nature and make a positive difference to the community. If you can't volunteer, just come and enjoy the mosaic of grassland, woodland, scrub and wetland the park has to offer.

tcv.org.uk/urbanecology/stave-hill-ecological-park ♥*Behind Bacons College, Timber Pond Road, SE16 6AX* **FREE** *24 hours* *Rotherhithe, Canada Water* *There is wheelchair access*

LAVENDER POND
Walk over the water for a unique view

Lavender Pond is built on the former Surrey Commercial Docks and was formerly an expanse of shallow water where timber was stored to keep it from drying out. The ecology park was created in 1981 with the aim of recalling the kind of wetland habitats that had once existed on the banks of the Thames. A network of ramps criss-cross the wetlands and water, so you can peer close-up at animals and plants. There's a varied selection of courses and activities on offer, from bat and fungi walks to moth evenings.

tcv.org.uk/urbanecology/urban-ecology-sites/ lavender-pond-nature-park ♥*Lavender Road, SE16 5DZ* **FREE** *Opening times vary – contact the park for details (020 7237 9165)* *Rotherhithe, Canada Water* *There is wheelchair access*

FARMS

London's first city farm was set up in Kentish Town in 1972 and inspired many others. In every corner of the city you'll find animals grazing and crops growing on scraps of land saved from development, wedged in between railway lines or set aside by councils with vision.

London's farms are the places where city kids are introduced to the sights, sounds and smells of the country and where adults relive their childhood days; most have education at their heart, teaching our children – and us – about agriculture, food production, ecology and even rural arts.

They're a good place to visit on a cold day, with barns to duck into, cafes (often serving produce fresh from the furrows) to warm up in and with plenty to occupy little hands. Make your way to one early in the year to see lambs being born and the first shoots of spring, or late in the year for real-life nativity scenes.

An alpaca enjoys a tasty snack at Mudchute Farm.

VAUXHALL CITY FARM
Rural life in the urban jungle

The most central city farm, Vauxhall's mission is to bring nature to everyone, regardless of their physical capabilities. They specialize in educational and therapeutic activities, including Riding for the Disabled sessions. Their riding school is open to everyone, with lessons, sessions and Own a Pony Days, all taking place in a large paddock set in Vauxhall Pleasure Gardens. If you're not after equine kicks, there are plenty of other animals around, including goats, rabbits, alpacas and ferrets and an ecology garden with a wormery, aviary and stag beetle nursery.

vauxhallcityfarm.org *165 Tyers St, SE11 5HS* **FREE** *Tuesday–Sunday 10.30 a.m.–4 p.m.* *Vauxhall* *There is wheelchair access*

DEEN CITY FARM
Swooping owls and soft alpacas

Right next to Morden Hall Park, Deen City Farm's five acres are home to cows, alpacas, an aviary, owls and turkeys, as well as gardens and a riding school. People of all ages flock to ride at weekends, with a quick trot around the paddock costing only £2 for kids. Don't miss the breathtaking daily owl-flying sessions, the regular animal-handling events, where kids can stroke smaller beasts, or your chance to help feed the pigs, then stop off at the cafe for a slice of home-made cake or buy some local produce from the farm shop.

deencityfarm.co.uk ♥*39 Windsor Ave, SW19 2RR* **FREE** ⏱ *Tuesday–Sunday 10 a.m.–6.30 p.m.* 🚇*Colliers Wood* ♿ *There is wheelchair access*

SURREY DOCKS FARM
Sparks fly in the working forge

This 2.2-acre farm in Rotherhithe has plenty of animals big and small to scratch and pet, and some beautiful planted areas. The dye garden is especially interesting; plants traditionally used to colour fabrics grow here, ready to be used in the popular dyeing workshops held on the farm. The farm has a working forge where you can take courses in the elemental skill of creating metal objects and runs popular beekeeping lessons. The Piccalilli Caff is a cosy hideaway if the weather is a little grim.

surreydocksfarm.org.uk ♥*Rotherhithe St, SE16 5ET* **FREE** ⏱ *10 a.m.–5 p.m. Cafe closed on Mondays* 🚇*Canada Water* ♿ *There is wheelchair access*

MUDCHUTE PARK AND FARM
Acres of space and city views

Situated on a huge, 32-acre site with iconic views of Canary Wharf and the City, Mudchute Farm feels luxuriously spacious for a city farm, with meadows and large paddocks big enough for its alpacas, donkeys and long-horned sheep to run around in. Pigs grunt and snuffle in the mud and ponies have plenty of space to gallop in. Little kids will love the petting area, full of cute, cuddly animals. It's big enough to spend all day here – take a picnic and breathe in lungfuls of fresh air. There's a large cafe, farm shop and a traditional Cockney fish shop, where you can buy fresh jellied eels, cockles, prawns and whelks.

---

mudchute.org *Pier Street, Isle of Dogs, E14 3HP* **FREE** *9 a.m.–5 p.m.* *Mudchute DLR* *There is wheelchair access*

FORTY HALL FARM
Try your hand at farming life

Forty Hall Farm is part of the eighteenth-century Forty Hall estate and is run by Capel Manor College, a further-education centre. It's big, beautiful and feels like a 'real' farm. There are walls and ruins to walk around, an orchard, an organic, commercial vineyard and a market garden that sells vegetables through a box scheme. There are also rare-breed animals to see and smell. The farm runs a busy programme of one-day courses in countryside skills, including coppicing, hedge-laying, mushroom hunting and foraging. The college also hosts regular large-scale special events, from the Beer and Blues Festival, which mixes storming live music with real ale and ciders, and September's City Harvest Festival, which brings together the finest produce and most beautiful animals from farms across London.

fortyhallfarm.org.uk ♥ *Forty Hall Farm, Forty Hill, EN2 9HA* £ *children free*
🕐 *Wednesday–Sunday 11 a.m.–4 p.m.* 🚉 *Enfield Chase, Enfield Town, Gordon Hill and Turkey Street overground* ♿ *There is wheelchair access*

STEPNEY CITY FARM
Country arts and crafts preserved

The sounds, sights and smells of a blacksmith at work are viscerally impressive; see one sparking, banging and clanging on-site at Stepney's Rural Arts Centre. There's also a woodworker and a potter and they all lead classes for adults and children in crafts treasured and preserved at this working farm. The farm is also home to animals large and small, a Saturday Farmers' Market and an award-winning cafe. It's a place that is well loved and well used by the local community and feels warm and inviting.

---

*stepneycityfarm.org ♀Stepney Way, E1 3DG **FREE** Tuesday–Sunday 10 a.m.–4 p.m. Stepney Green There is wheelchair access*

WOODLANDS FARM
Farm animals meet wild beasts

This big (89-acre) working farm is on the fringes of London, but well worth a visit. There are white cattle, Shetland ponies and rare-breed pigs, as well as smaller animals. It's a great place to spot wildlife too; wander around its meadows, ancient woodland and ponds to find voles, birds and butterflies. There are regular guided walks and family events, including the hugely popular and heart-warming lambing days in spring.

---

*thewoodlandsfarmtrust.org ♀331 Shooters Hill, DA16 3RP **FREE** Tuesday–Sunday 9.30 a.m.–4.30 p.m. and Bank Holiday Mondays Welling overground There is wheelchair access*

KENTISH TOWN CITY FARM
Ride a horse as trains rumble by

The first of London's city farms, this little haven is built in and around Gospel Oak overground. There are over fifty animals, including chickens, geese, goats, a pig and a cow, but the real stars of the show are the horses. There's a floodlit, outdoor paddock, around which the children of the area ride – weekend trots are £2 a go.

⟨ ktcityfarm.org.uk ⏺ 1 Cressfield Close, off Grafton Road, NW5 4BN **FREE** ⏲ 9 a.m.–5 p.m. ⦿ Kentish Town, Gospel Oak ♿ There is wheelchair access

FREIGHTLINERS CITY FARM
Going loco in N7

So named because the animals were originally housed in old railway goods vans (there are still one or two on site), this farm is a neat, family-friendly place, perfect for little ones to wander around independently. There's a small duck pond, lots of rabbits and a trail through the dinky fields, with animal surprises around every corner. The cafe is especially good; it's housed in a fresh-feeling, sustainable building with a covered balcony and serves delicious vegetarian food, much of which is made from ingredients grown on the farm. It's adjacent to a park with a great playground – make a day of it.

freightlinersfarm.org.uk _Sheringham Rd, N7 8PF_ **FREE** _Autumn–winter 10 a.m.–4 p.m.; spring–summer 10 a.m.–4.45 p.m._ _Highbury and Islington_ _There is wheelchair access_

SPITALFIELDS CITY FARM
See goats run through the East End

Follow the sound of the braying donkey from Brick Lane and you'll find yourself at this urban farm, set up by squatters in the 1970s. See pigs, sheep, chickens and cows and explore the ponds, wildlife and vegetable gardens. The highlight of the year is the annual Oxford and Cambridge Goat Race (see page 134), which takes place on the same day as the official Boat Race. Other popular events include pumpkin carving, sheep shearing and a 'moosic' festival.

spitalfieldscityfarm.org ♀*Buxton Street, E1 5AR* **FREE** ⓣ*Tuesday–Sunday 10 a.m.–4 p.m.* 🚇*Whitechapel* ♿*There is wheelchair access*

SHOPS AND MARKETS

If you don't have time to get to your nearest park, let alone the actual countryside, allow rural life to come to you. Some of the home counties' best producers visit the city's markets every week, bringing courgettes still wet with dew, mushrooms plucked from meadows and shining, fresh fish. There are farmers' markets across town, thronged weekly with visitors, offering ingredients to inspire you, as well as faster-food hits to cure your hangover.

There are more permanent places to explore, too. Shops, stacked with tempting wares you might expect to find only in village stores or town markets, or things to make your home feel more like a country manor than a small flat. Or indulge your love of the soil at a garden centre, from the brutally smart to the scrubbily helpful. Even the smallest balcony can be transformed into a green oasis with a few pots and some trailing vines, or strike out and get supplies to turn your house into an urban smallholding. The not-so-green-fingered will enjoy soaking up the atmosphere while they sample the home-made cakes in some of the city's most beautiful and verdant cafes.

Tasty treats on offer at Borough Market.

COLUMBIA ROAD FLOWER MARKET
Blooming into life every Sunday

Once a week, Columbia Road blossoms into the most beautiful, fragrant street in town, as the flower sellers set out their stalls. Track the seasons by the plants on offer: yolk-yellow daffodils trumpeting spring's arrival, tall tulips standing ramrod straight, decadent roses tumbling rudely in summer and red berry-studded greenery lit by glittering lights in drizzly December. The flowers here seem bigger and more fragrant than any other in London; it's the Hall of Fame of blooms. Wander around the road's shops too, for chic homewares, vintage fabrics and home-made confections and coffee from Cakehole. Linger around the market near closing time to try to catch some bargains.

columbiaroad.info *Columbia Rd, E2 7RG* *8 a.m.–3 p.m., Sundays only*
Bethnal Green, Hoxton overground *There is wheelchair access*

CHEGWORTH FARM SHOP
Fresh produce in the heart of Notting Hill

First established as a stand in Borough Market, Chegworth Farm Shop on Kensington Church Street stocks farm-fresh vegetables, chutneys, organic flour and stunning fresh flowers, as well as every last variety of their sunset-hued, signature range of fresh farm-pressed juices. Incongruously rustic on a street lined with antique shops and estate agents, you'll find the ingredients to cook up pies and puddings. Upstairs, there's a coffee-and-juice bar perfect for people-watching.

chegworthvalley.com 221 Kensington Church Street, W8 7LX Monday–Saturday 8 a.m.–8 p.m., Sunday 9 a.m.–6 p.m. Notting Hill Gate There is wheelchair access

CHELSEA GARDENER
Upmarket greenery for modern gardens

Need a hit of chlorophyll while walking along the King's Road? Duck into the Chelsea Gardener for a chi-chi blast of greenery, as manicured as a debutante's nails. This is gardening nirvana for those who love order; a well-clipped box hedge, obedient olive trees in pots, brutally efficient outdoor sofas. Hard as it is to imagine the residents of SW3 getting their hands dirty, you'll find compost, pots and trowels here too.

chelseagardener.com 125 Sydney St, London SW3 6NR Monday–Saturday 10 a.m.– 6 p.m., Sunday 12–6 p.m. Sloane Square There is wheelchair access

BOROUGH MARKET
The best in show of farmers' markets

Not only does a stroll through Borough Market bring you the sights and smells of the British countryside – pheasants hanging from nails, enormous game pies, tables groaning under luscious pumpkins – but it can also transport you to rural Europe. Find hand-carved legs of Italian acorn-fed pigs at Bianca e Mora, nutty manchego cheese at Brindisa, or delicately scented macarons at Comptoir Gourmand. Make leisurely circuits of the cavernous, undercover venue, picking as you go: an oyster to slurp here, a sample of sharp, dark pickle there. Then take your haul of goodies to the south bank for the most superior of picnics.

---

boroughmarket.org.uk *8 Southwark St, SE1 1TL* *Monday–Tuesday limited market 10 a.m.–5 p.m., Wednesday–Thursday 10 a.m.–5 p.m., Friday 10 a.m.–6 p.m., Saturday 8 a.m.–5 p.m.* *London Bridge* *There is wheelchair access*

MEAT N16 BUTCHER AND DELICATESSEN
No beef with this beef

Despite only opening in 2011, Meat N16 is already part of the Stoke Newington establishment. It's a thoroughly modern butcher, but with a traditional feel. Selling high-quality, free-range meats from UK farms, the incredibly knowledgeable staff are happy to advise and demystify the meat-buying process and recommend accompanying wines from their eclectic wine room. The shop has a cellar which, when there aren't handmade sausages being made in there, hosts courses in butchery or meat preparation. There's even a small garden for summer barbecues.

---

meatlondon.co.uk *104 Stoke Newington Church Street, N16 0LA* *Tuesday–Friday 9.30 a.m.–7 p.m., Saturday 9 a.m.–5 p.m., Sunday 9.30 a.m.–4 p.m. Closed Mondays* *Stoke Newington overground* *There is wheelchair access*

WALTHAMSTOW FARMERS' MARKET
A warmhearted welcome awaits

Walthamstow market has a real community feel; there's a big crowd of regular customers and frequent family fun days, with kids' activities and games. Producers include Giggly Pig, whose sausages come from free-range Romford hogs, Happy Cow, who sell unpasteurised milk and cream, and the locals' favourite, Ted's Veg.

lfm.org.uk/markets/walthamstow/ ♀Town Square by Selbourne Walk Shopping Centre, off the High Street, E17 7JN Sunday 10 a.m.–3 p.m. Walthamstow Central There is wheelchair access

HORNIMAN FARMERS' MARKET
As eccentric and varied as the exhibits in the museum

Many of London's farmers' markets are operated by a handful of companies, but this foodfest feels truly independent. Held in the extremely pretty gardens of the Horniman Museum, you'll find smoked fish, hot soups, organic meat and vegetables, pies and handmade, fresh sushi. It's difficult to resist a post-nibble wander around the quirky, fun and free museum. A very satisfying day out.

horniman.ac.uk/visit/events/horniman-farmers-market ♀100 London Road, SE23 3PQ Saturday 9 a.m.–1.30 p.m. Forest Hill overground There is wheelchair access

LIBERTY LONDON
Live like a lord in foliage-sprigged fabrics

The impressive halls of the Liberty of London store house some of the most luxurious goods in the UK. However, with its beamed exterior and panelled interior, the place feels like the grandest market-town department store imaginable. This is where squires from the shires come to select next decade's Barbour jacket, where those who own country piles find curtains and carpets and where mere mortals can get a whiff of the country by burying their heads in racks of Liberty-print, flowery silks.

libertylondon.com Regent St, W1B 5AH 10 a.m.–8 p.m., Sunday 12 p.m.–6 p.m. Oxford Circus There is wheelchair access

PIMLICO ROAD FARMERS' MARKET
A sweet-smelling piazza of epicurean wonders

Held in a gorgeous, leafy square, in summer this Saturday-morning market feels almost like mainland Europe. The sweet aromas of M&R Morton's roses waft across the piazza and Phil's Pesto and Pasta could compete with Italy's best. Look out for feathered partridge and pheasants hanging over stalls when in season.

lfm.org.uk/markets/pimlico-road/ Orange Square, corner of Pimlico Road and Ebury Street, SW1W 8UT Saturday 9 a.m.–1 p.m. Sloane Square There is wheelchair access

PETERSHAM NURSERIES
Stunning food, but don't forget about the plants

Perhaps most famous for its star-studded-yet-earth-floored cafe, Petersham Nurseries was carved out of the grounds of the elegant Petersham House in the 1970s. It's tucked away down a pretty alley adjacent to the National Trust's Petersham Meadows and stocked with beautiful, flawless plants, all displayed artfully on old carts and wooden trestle tables. It's the kind of place that, if you don't have a garden, will have you joining the waiting list at your nearest allotment and if you do have outdoor space, heading home with armfuls of greenery and a huge smile.

petershamnurseries.com ♀ Church Lane, off Petersham Road, TW10 7AB
🕐 Monday–Saturday 9 a.m.–5 p.m., Sunday 11 a.m.–5 p.m. 🚌 Twickenham overground ♿ There is wheelchair access

THE GOOD LIFE

With rents rising hourly and space in the city becoming more squeezed, it's increasingly tempting to sell up and move to the country. However, you don't need to ditch your 020 code for a self-sufficient smallholding – there are many ways to live the good life while staying put. There are alternatives to supermarket-bought vegetables: grow your own on an allotment, go foraging for wild food in the city's parks, or pick your own. Once you've gone off-grid foodwise, it's a small step to keeping chickens or even making your own cheese.

Many of us are becoming more politically aware about where our food comes from; the Abundance movement redistributes fruit from unloved trees and Organiclea aims to give the community back the means to grow and distribute food in an ethical way. Meanwhile, the Guerrilla Gardening gang are brightening up our day-to-day lives by flower-bombing forgotten spaces and reclaiming our roundabouts. Why not join them?

Learn to make your own cheese with Wildes Cheese.

PARKSIDE PICK YOUR OWN FARM
Be inspired by the freshest fruit and vegetables

Work up an appetite in the sun as you pick your own fruit and vegetables. Parkside is an enormous farm close to Trent Park, with raspberries, sweetcorn, marrows, redcurrants and spinach bursting from the ground. They even grow their strawberries on raised 'tabletops' to save your back. It's a happy place; kids run around stuffing fruit into their mouths, there's loads of open space and the shop sells meringues and chocolate dipping sauce, so you can tuck into your spoils on the tables set outside. It's a healthier, outdoor Wonka Factory, full of treats and surprises and all the fresh produce is certain to inspire you to experiment in the kitchen. Take your biggest basket.

---

parksidefarmpyo.co.uk ♀*Hadley Road, EN2 8LA* £*Priced per kg* ⏰*Open June–September (dependent on weather) weekdays 10 a.m.–5 p.m., weekends 9 a.m.–5 p.m., days according to season.* 🚇*Oakwood, Enfield Chase overground* ♿*Accessible*

CHICKEN KEEPING AT HEN CORNER
Fresh eggs and friendly pecks

The joy of freshly laid eggs, contented clucks and some friendly pecks are the little things that make keeping hens such a pleasure. It's possible to keep chickens in a small garden or on an allotment; find out how at one of Hen Corner's poultry-keeping courses. The courses are held at Sara Ward's end-of-terrace house in Brentford, which, with twenty hens, two colonies of bees, fruit trees and a micro-bakery, is an inspirational urban smallholding.

---

hencorner.com/courses/ £*Keeping chickens courses start at £45* 🚇*Brentford* ♿*Accessible*

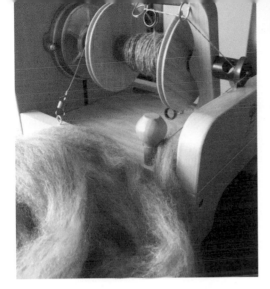

WEAVING AND SPINNING
The most relaxing spinning class in town

Taking wool straight from the sheep and turning it into fabric is a dying (and dyeing) art, but it's kept alive at the Handweavers Studio & Gallery. Find out about warps and wefts and twists and colour at one of their regular classes in weaving, spinning, dyeing and other fibre crafts. Their Introduction to Weaving and Spinning courses are perfect for those wanting an introduction to the skill, while there are plenty of workshops for more experienced makers, and a rainbow of yarns and fibres plus equipment also available for a delicious browse.

handweavers.co.uk ♀140 Seven Sisters Road, N7 7NS £ ⓘ Shop open Monday–Saturday 10 a.m.–6 p.m. Finsbury Park ♿ There is easy wheelchair access to the ground-floor shop and toilet

ORGANICLEA
A Lea Valley workers' cooperative

Organiclea's vision is a food system under the control of the people, providing a fair income to food producers and using ecologically sound methods. What this means in practical terms is a fruit and veg box scheme with produce supplied by local growers and small-scale farmers, practical support for community gardens and a series of courses, open days and one-off events. They're good people, working towards an excellent cause, and there are plenty of practical ways to get involved; sign up for one of their weekly veg boxes, take one of their courses or sell your surplus produce to them. Visit on one of their monthly open days for inspiration.

organiclea.org.uk ♀115 Hawkwood Crescent, Chingford, E4 7UH ♿ Not fully wheelchair accessible

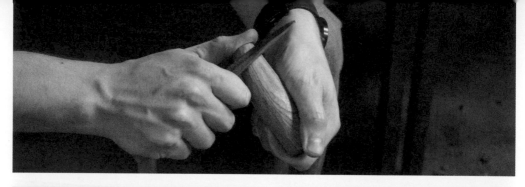

WOODWORKING COURSES AT THE GREEN WOOD GUILD
Whittle your way to contentment

Woodworking brings us closer to the natural world and back to simpler times. Based at the Rural Arts Centre at Stepney Farm, the Green Wood Guild use traditional hand tools to work with fresh green wood straight from the tree. The centre offers courses in whittling, woodworking, furniture-making and, excitingly, axe-smithing and blade-making. You might end up with a spatula, a stool or a carving knife, or even a new skill to obsess over. Try an introductory workshop to get a taste for your chosen craft.

thegreenwoodguild.com ♀ Rural Arts Centre, Stepney City Farm, Stepney Way, E1 3DG £ Courses start from £35 Stepney Green, Limehouse There is wheelchair access

CHEESE-MAKING AT WILDES CHEESE
Uncover the mysteries of rennet and curd

Cheese has a reputation for being fiddly and difficult to make. Wildes Cheese are based on an industrial estate in Tottenham, make their own range of cheeses and are passionate about dairy products. They run one-day and evening classes that teach cheese-making without the need for any special equipment. You'll go home with a soft curd and small fresh specimen to ripen at home, plus a head full of cheesespiration.

⬥ wildescheese.co.uk/collections/cheese-making-classes ♀ Queen St, N17 8JA ⊕ Friday 10 a.m.–6 p.m., Saturday 8 a.m.–5 p.m., Sunday 10 a.m.–3 p.m., Monday 8 a.m.–5 p.m., Thursday 10 a.m.–5 p.m. Closed Tuesday and Wednesday ▣ White Hart Lane overground ♿ There is wheelchair access

FORAGE LONDON
Find your own food for free

Writer John Rensten used to run a pub in London, The Green, which pioneered putting foraged food on the menu. He now runs courses and leads walks in the capital, ferreting out fungi and showing city-dwellers how to find food for free. His company's wanders include uncovering the edible delights of Hampstead Heath; a walk foraging for wild medicinal flora; and exploring the Tower Hamlets Nature Reserve looking for delicious plants with a healthy side order of nature trailing. You'll be inspired to make foraging for food a regular habit: nothing beats getting up early to find chestnuts in the mist, picking sloes dripping with dew, or gathering leaves of slippery and pungent wild garlic, then taking them home to your kitchen.

⬥ foragelondon.co.uk £ Courses start from £30

ABUNDANCE
Superhero redistributors of the fruit glut

The nationwide Abundance movement formed around ten years ago, aiming to harvest the UK's hidden and seasonal glut of produce. The UK imports 90 per cent of its fruit and 70 per cent of its vegetables, but there is still produce rotting on the trees in people's gardens and in the countryside. The network of Abundance groups across London works with local schools and other volunteers to map trees, pick fruit, make jam, juice and chutney to sell and raise money, or to give to food banks. Ealing Abundance produces industrial quantities of jam, Kensal to Kilburn works with local refugee groups, Belsize Park collaborates with the Transition movement and Haringey runs foraging walks alongside the harvesting.

abundancelondon.com

GUERRILLA GARDENING
Brightening up your neighbourhood one scrubby patch at a time

Richard Reynolds has been surreptitiously weeding and seeding London's neglected flower beds, roundabouts and patches of scruffy land since 2004 and now spearheads Britain's Guerrilla Gardening movement. He started tending flower beds neglected by the council after moving to a high-rise tower block in Elephant and Castle. With an army of volunteers, he now looks after a series of unloved patches of ground, including a huge raised bed the size of a tennis court on a traffic island near Lambeth North station. He often does talks and one-off events and his website is a hub for wannabe green terrorists – visit it for inspiration or to join a local group.

guerrillagardening.org

SPORTS AND ACTIVITIES

Sometimes it's not enough to be a passive absorber and observer of the more pleasant things around us. We want total immersion in the greener life, to take part in activities and maybe even keep fit while we're doing so. Playing a sport – non-strenuous, of course, and preferably one in which you can take part while holding a drink in one hand – is a pleasant way to spend a warm evening and even time spent watching a game helps you to unwind.

Embarking on a new, countryside-inspired hobby is rewarding and a practical way to keep rural arts alive. From horse riding to country dancing, there's something to soothe or inspire everyone. As a bonus, getting out and taking part in activities is a fine means to meet like-minded people as well as exploring Britain's (and further afield's) culture.

Paddleboarding on the Thames at sunset.

CRICKET
The gentlest sport to watch and play

The game that sums up rural Britain, there are cricket pitches across the capital, large and small. The huge greens of Lords and The Oval host international and county games; however, there are many smaller places to watch cricket where you'll be welcome to turn up with a picnic blanket and take in the game for free. Many teams are also actively looking for players; our favourite clubs are Crouch End, with its welcoming pavilion and views of Alexandra Palace, and Barnes, set next to the Thames. There's also a secret cricket pitch in the City, the Artillery Ground, open once a year for the public to look around, but whose army teams are often looking for non-serving members.

Crouch End cricket club: *crouchendcricket.com/*
Barnes cricket club: *barnescc.co.uk* The Artillery Ground: *hac.org.uk/home/about-the-hac/clubs-societies/hac-sports-clubs/cricket-club/*

PÉTANQUE
Summon up the spirit of the French countryside

The dink of steel on steel, the smell of Pernod and the warmth of summer sun on your back. Pétanque is the archetypal game of rural France, played in village squares across the country. In London, you'll find a little community based in Cleaver Square in Kennington, who gather to throw metal balls at a small wooden ball, to laugh and to have a drink or two. The London club welcome anyone to come and have a go and friendly players will get you up to speed on the rules and techniques. If you don't have a set of boules, borrow them from the nearby Prince of Wales pub.

---

londonpetanqueclub.com/ Cleaver Square, SE11 4EA **FREE** Summer (BST months): every Wednesday from 5 p.m. until dusk. Winter: first Saturday of every month; casual competition from 11 a.m. Kennington There is wheelchair access

GREEN GYMS
Get leaner, make the city greener

Indoor gyms are some of the harshest, most urban environments you'll find. However, there is a way to keep fit, get outside and make a difference to the local community. Green Gyms are outdoor ecology sessions held by The Conservation Volunteers. One week you might be sowing a meadow, the next digging a pond. The activities are selected to burn calories and increase fitness and the session includes a warm-up and cool-down. Plus you'll get a warm glow knowing you've contributed to making the city a more beautiful, wildlife-friendly place.

tcv.org.uk/greengym   Across London   **FREE**

PADDLEBOARDING
See the riverbank from a self-powered craft

Pottering along under your own steam is a quiet, meditative way to explore a waterway. Active 360's introductory classes will show you the basics of stand-up paddleboarding in locations across London, in Kew Bridge, Putney, Brentford and Paddington Lock. The section of river between Richmond and Putney is perhaps the most tranquil, all low-hanging trees and new angles on London vistas. There are places where, as you glide along with just the quiet plops of water voles and the occasional flap of a coot for company, you'll feel truly alone and immersed in a *Wind in the Willows* world.

active360.co.uk ♀*Locations across London* £ ♿*Call for access information (0203 3935 360)*

HORSE RIDING
Take an atmospheric canter through London's history

Riding a horse through the centre of London is a slightly surreal, but very pleasant, experience. Hyde Park Stables has five miles (8 km) of bridleways that run past some of London's most famous landmarks; the stables offer group rides, lessons and private gallops. Even if you're a novice, once you're on horseback it's easy to imagine yourself cantering across rolling fields rather than parkland – book a misty, autumnal morning session for maximum atmosphere and minimum tourist attention.

hydeparkstables.com ♀63 Bathurst Mews, W2 2SB £ ⊙Open 7.30 a.m.–6 p.m. ➡Lancaster Gate ♿Contact the stables for detailed access information (020 7723 2813)

ROWING
Whatever floats your boat

Taking a rowing boat for a glide around a lake is a very civilized, relaxing way to spend an hour and provides peace, even in the centre of town. The Regent's Park Boating Lake has boats and pedalos for hire; get a little closer to the ducks and take a spin around the island, or do a little light romancing in this beautiful setting. There's even a smaller lake with pedalos for children to hire, ideal for tiring them out during the school holidays.

royalparks.org.uk/parks/the-regents-park/things-to-see-and-do/sports-and-leisure/boat-and-pedalo-hire ♀Hanover Gate, The Regent's Park, NW1 4NU £ ⊙April–October 10.30 a.m.–6 p.m., children's lake open weekends, bank holidays and school holidays only ➡Regent's Park ♿Limited wheelchair access

MORRIS DANCING
Dare you keep your appointment with the bell-wearing men?

There's something a little sinister and Wicker Man-like about morris dancing. Perhaps it's the hooden horse figures that accompany some troupes, the relentless jangling bells or just the extreme jollity of the dancers. The origins of this ritual dancing, usually only performed by men, are lost, but it was revived at the beginning of the twentieth century during a drive to preserve the traditions of rural life. The London Pride club was founded in the 1930s and meet through autumn and winter in order to perform at shows and events during the spring and summer. They also run country dancing sessions fortnightly at RADA in Bloomsbury, where women are welcome.

lpmm.org.uk Haverstock School on Haverstock Hill, NW3 2BQ Autumn and winter school terms, Tuesdays 7 p.m.–9 p.m. Chalk Farm There is wheelchair access

LONDON SKITTLES
Build them up just to knock them down

The Hampstead Lawn Billiards and Skittles Club has been playing this ancient form of bowling in the cellar of the Freemasons' Arms in Hampstead since 1933 – prior to that, it was played in the pub's outhouse. It's a peculiar game, where competitors aim to knock down ninepins with a 'cheese' (a hardwood object in the shape of a cheese) and today the club is the last known bastion of the sport. Club nights are on Tuesdays and novices are welcome to try their hand at the sport and drink a few pints with the regulars.

*londonskittles.co.uk 32 Downshire Hill, NW3 1NT **FREE** Taster sessions Tuesdays 8 p.m.–11 p.m. Hampstead, Hampstead Heath overground Limited wheelchair access*

COUNTRY DANCING AND SINGING AT CECIL SHARP HOUSE

Learn about English traditions in the most beautiful of settings

Home to the English Folk Dance and Song Society, the strains of fiddles, unaccompanied voices and stamping feet regularly float out of Cecil Sharp House. Its wood-panelled rooms play host to ceilidhs, lectures, courses and concerts, as the Society keeps centuries-old English folk traditions alive through vibrant performances. Join them to celebrate May Day, take a course in country dancing or join in a choir workshop. Think of it as London's village hall and use it often.

cecilsharphouse.org ♀*2 Regent's Park Road, NW1 7AY* £ *Open dependent on event. Cafe open Monday–Saturday 10 a.m.–5 p.m., Sunday–Tuesday 6 p.m.–11 p.m.* *Camden Town* *There is wheelchair access*

PUBS

Step over the threshold of the right London pub and you can be instantly transported out of town and into the depths of rural Britain. From places with balmy, walled beer gardens to wood-panelled snugs, or inns that serve the best game pies in the country, the sheer variety of London's watering holes can whisk you into the shires. Find a place with a crackling fire, perfect for rainy Sunday-evening drinking, or an inn overlooking a duck pond or heath. Go for a stroll, work up an appetite (all of the pubs listed serve food) and a thirst – and enjoy.

Visit the Flask, Hampstead, for a
drink in one of London's cosiest pubs.

THE SEVEN STARS, HOLBORN
Where legal eagles come to perch

Four centuries old and with bags of charm and character, this pub is a rare retreat in the heart of Lincoln's Inn's legal-land. Feeling more like a tavern in a market town than a pub in the heart of the capital, it's full of wonderful clutter and serves hearty, home-cooked food. Keep your ears open and you might overhear some great court-related gossip.

♀53–54 Carey St, WC2A 2JB ☎020 7242 8521 ⏱11 a.m.–11 p.m., Saturday 12 p.m.–11 p.m., Sunday 12 p.m.–10 p.m. 🚇Chancery Lane, Temple ♿Limited wheelchair access

THE NARROWBOAT, ISLINGTON
A water-side idyll

Overlooking the Regent's Canal in Islington, The Narrowboat is the ideal place to appreciate the beauty and calming qualities of the water, with a glass of something cold in your hand. In summer, sit out on the glass-fronted terrace, perfect for wildlife-spotting or towpath people-watching. The picturesque narrowboats on the banks of the waterway will have you dreaming of a simpler, more mobile life.

🖊thenarrowboatpub.com ♀119 St Peter's Street, N1 8PZ ☎020 7400 6003 ⏱11 a.m.–11 p.m., Fridays and Saturdays 11 a.m.–12 a.m. 🚇Angel ♿There is wheelchair access

THE CROOKED BILLET, WIMBLEDON
Sprawl on the grass to enjoy your drink

The Crooked Billet feels so much like a village pub transplanted to the city, it can come as a bit of a shock to spot a red London bus when you emerge. It's situated right on the edge of Wimbledon Common, where you can take out your pints in the summer and recline on their rugs and deckchairs. In winter, the fires are cosy and provide glow and warmth after a long trudge across the Common. It's run by one of the friendliest landlords in town, too.

thecrookedbilletwimbledon.com 14–15 Crooked Billet, SW19 4RQ 020 8946 4942 11 a.m.–11 p.m., Friday and Saturday 11 a.m.–12 p.m. Wimbledon overground There is wheelchair access

THE WHITE HART, BARNES
Watch boats glide by at this Thames-side pub

There's been a pub on this site since 1660, although the current White Hart was built in 1899. The big selling point of the place is its views from the south bank across the River Thames. This is leafy territory in which to spot coots, moorhens and swans gliding by as you sit in the Terrace Kitchen. It's the perfect place from which to watch the Boat Race or, in winter, for nursing warming glasses of mulled wine, with blankets and hot-water bottles provided on the balcony.

whitehartbarnes.co.uk The Terrace, Riverside, SW13 0NR 020 8876 5177 11 a.m.–11 p.m., Friday and Saturday 11 a.m.–12 a.m., Sunday 12 p.m.–11 p.m. Barnes Bridge overground Limited wheelchair access

THE NAGS HEAD, KNIGHTSBRIDGE
Turn off your mobile or get an earful

If it's the countryside's patchy network coverage and the full attention of your friends that you crave, this tiny watering hole has a mobile ban that's stringently in place. A quirky tavern with a real fire and walls crammed with paraphernalia, it's insulated from its well-heeled surroundings and hidden down a rather beautiful mews street. Don't miss the vintage peep show and beware the sternness of the landlord if you break the house rules.

♀53 Kinnerton St, SW1X 8ED ☎020 7235 1135 ⏲11 a.m.–11 p.m. 🚇Knightsbridge ♿Limited wheelchair access

THE ORANGE TREE, TOTTERIDGE
Drink on the village green courtesy of this bucolic boozer

This pub pretty much sums up rural idyll. It's in delightful Totteridge and backs on to a cricket pitch and village green. Take a pint outside and sit next to the small pond and you could be in a small Sussex village rather than a few minutes' walk away from an underground station.

♲theorangetreetotteridge.co.uk ♀7 Totteridge Village, N20 8NX ☎020 8343 7031 ⏲11 a.m.–11 p.m., Friday 11 a.m.–11.30 p.m., Saturday 9 a.m.–11.30 p.m., Sunday 9 a.m.–10.30 p.m. 🚇Totteridge and Whetstone ♿There is wheelchair access

THE FLASK, HAMPSTEAD
Cosy up after a long hike on the Heath

Perfect for a warming glass of red wine or a cracking Sunday roast after a long walk on the Heath, the Flask is one of the most atmospheric pubs in London. There's been a pub here for at least 300 years and the dark wood panelling and beautiful glass screens feel steeped in history. Stick to the public or saloon bars for a sense of the olden days, or head to the conservatory for a little more light.

theflaskhampstead.co.uk *14 Flask Walk, NW3 1HE* *020 7435 4580* *11 a.m.–11 p.m., Sunday 12 p.m.–10.30 p.m.* *Hampstead* *There is wheelchair access*

THE WHITE SWAN, TWICKENHAM
Watch your feet at high tide

Perched idyllically near Eel Pie Island on the gently sloping banks of the Thames, the White Swan has one of the finest beer gardens in London. Although it does have a tendency to flood at high tide, this free house has steadfastly remained here since the seventeenth century. While away an hour or two in the sun underneath the flower baskets outside, or spend a cosy winter afternoon tucked beside one of their real fires. You won't want to budge.

whiteswantwickenham.co.uk ♀ Riverside, Twickenham, TW1 3DN ☎ 020 8744 2951 ⏱ Sunday–Monday 11 a.m.–10.30 p.m., Tuesday–Saturday 11 a.m.–11 p.m. ♿ Limited wheelchair access

THE SUN INN, BARNES
A village pub inside and outside

Perfectly situated, the Sun Inn is a delightful pub overlooking a village green.On a sunny day, with a pint of real ale and a handmade Scotch egg, it feels like you could be in deepest Yorkshire. The Thames is only a short stroll away – work off your indulgences with a walk along the towpath.

thesuninnbarnes.co.uk ♀ 7 Church Road, SW13 9HE ☎ 020 8876 5256 ⏱ 11 a.m.–11 p.m., Thursday and Friday 11 a.m.–12 p.m., Saturday 10 a.m.–12 p.m., Sunday 12 p.m.–11 p.m. 🚃 Barnes Bridge overground ♿ There is wheelchair access

THE TELEGRAPH, PUTNEY HEATH

Trees surround this family-friendly place to drink

A sign outside the Telegraph declares the place to be 'the country pub in London' – and it's not wrong. Set in the heart of Putney Heath, with green views and a rather inviting leafy garden to boot, it's extremely child-and-pet friendly and a lovely place for a relaxed drink or Sunday roast. Book a table for a post-heath-ramble lunch.

thetelegraphputney.co.uk Telegraph Rd, SW15 3TU 020 8788 2011 12 p.m.–11 p.m., Sunday 12 p.m.–9 p.m. East Putney, Putney overground There is wheelchair access

THE WINDMILL, MAYFAIR
The upper-est of crusts

There aren't many foods more country than a really good pie and this pub serves up some of the best. Their steak pie has won awards but it's their seasonal varieties that make our mouths water – try oxtail, rabbit or venison. If you're a real fan, sign up to join their pie club. Unusually for Mayfair, there's outside space in which to drink – a hidden roof terrace, the pub's 'Secret Garden'. Try a homegrown herb and fruit cocktail.

windmillmayfair.co.uk 6/8 Mill Street, W1S 2AZ 0207 491 8050 11.45 a.m.–11 p.m., Saturday 12 p.m.–11 p.m., Sunday 12 p.m.–6 p.m. Oxford Circus Limited wheelchair access

VILLAGES

London, as history books will never tire of reminding us, was formerly made up of a series of villages. Their boundaries thickened and blurred, covering the green spaces between them, until they became a whole city – a city that's still swallowing up smaller places today. However, the bone structure of these villages remain and pockets of London still feel like small conurbations, market towns and even ports, each with its own unique character. In these places you might find village greens, independent shops, church towers and, most importantly, community spirit. Head to one of these places for an afternoon's wander, but be warned – the urge to stay there permanently may take hold.

Have a wander down Flask Walk, in Hampstead, to feel that you have really escaped London's busy streets.

DULWICH VILLAGE
Gracious living in the suburbs

Dulwich Village's Georgian, Victorian and Edwardian houses were made a conservation area in 1968 and it's a leafy idyll with green spaces that include Dulwich Park with its boating lake, winter garden and vegetable garden and Dulwich Wood. Dulwich Picture Gallery was the world's first public art gallery and is set in wide-lawned gardens, while the nearby quirky Horniman Museum is a hugely entertaining place to visit on a rainy day. Walk along the main street of Dulwich Village for the gentlest of shopping sprees: Romeo Jones delicatessen sells locally produced honey, Village Books is great for browsing and Bartleys Flowers is the place for elegant blooms and the most stylish bouquets.

North Dulwich, West Dulwich overground

GREENWICH
Hello, sailors!

Feeling more like an eighteenth-century port town than a metropolitan borough, Greenwich is alive with history. The masts of the Cutty Sark dominate its skyline, a pointy reminder of the proximity of the river. Wander through its streets uncovering treasures in the charming undercover market (while sampling the delicious street food) and secret enclaves – Gloucester Circus is the most picturesque. Its museums are winning places to spend a few hours: the Maritime Museum's overhaul has made it a hit with children and adults alike; the Cutty Sark's dramatic, below-hull gallery is modern and fun; and the Observatory is an elegant building, filled with the secrets of the cosmos. Add a touch of eeriness to your trip with a mosey through the dark and echoing foot tunnel that runs under the Thames, opened in 1902.

🚌 *Greenwich DLR and overground*

CROUCH END
Arty, independent and self-sufficient

Crouch End's distance from tube stations and geographical position have isolated it a little from the hustle of London, and it still retains its bohemian heart. The north end is bounded by the green slopes of Alexandra Palace Park, while Queen's Wood's twisted trunks and shady spaces abut the west. Local shops on the Broadway provide every provision you might need: mouthwatering bread from Dunn's Bakery, fresh fish from Walter Purkis & Sons and game meats from Freemans the butchers. Locals drink in the Haringey Arms, while recent arrivals head for the ornate-ceilings at the Queens. The ex-British Legion social club Earl Haig Hall acts as a village hall, with a bar, pub quiz, live theatre, baby and toddler groups and yoga classes.

Finsbury Park, Highgate, Hornsey overground

RICHMOND HILL
Drink in the incredible verdant views

Sandwiched between a bucolic section of the Thames and the enormous spaces of Richmond Park, Richmond Hill is greedily green. The view from the top of the hill across Terrace Gardens is the only one in England to be protected by an act of Parliament: it's spectacular, with trees undulating into the distance, meadows and islets in the river, all fading to a khaki blur, unspoiled as far as you can see. There are huge houses here: Clarence House, the Royal Star and Garter Home and Halford House. Retire to the Roebuck for a pint, or head down the hill to Petersham Nurseries for an artfully rustic meal. You may even bump into local residents Pete Townshend and Mick Jagger, who have houses overlooking the gorgeous vistas.

Richmond overground

HIGHGATE
Join the village green preservation society

However you approach Highgate Village, you'll have to climb a hill, whether it's the crawl up Highgate Hill from Archway, a brisk climb up Southwood Lane from Highgate underground station, or the wind up past Highgate Cemetery from Hampstead Heath. Once at the top, your reward is fresh air and extremely pleasant environs. There are clusters of bow-fronted shops, a picturesque church and the sun-dappled expanse of Pond Square, where, nine times out of ten, you'll spot Ray Davies from The Kinks strolling around. Head to The Duke's Head for a pint of real ale or a gin cocktail made with Sacred, a spirit distilled just around the corner.

🚇 *Highgate, Archway*

STOKE NEWINGTON
Visit the People's Republic of Stokey

Stoke Newington's history of radical politics (Communist Party meetings were held in its town hall and the Stoke Newington Eight were arrested here for suspected involvement in the Angry Brigade bombings) still echoes a little today, most notably in the all-day political discussions held in the Rochester Castle pub. Although the area is now calmer and more monied than in its squatter-and-warehouse past, it retains a fiercely independent spirit: there are few chain stores here, plus community gardens, regular flea markets and a smattering of independent music venues. Clissold Park provides wonderful green space, with a mini zoo and paddling pool, while Abney Park Cemetery (see page 55) is accessible directly from the main drag of Church Street. Find great fish and chips at Sutton and Sons, or head down Kingsland Road for bargain, fresh Turkish food.

Stoke Newington overground

BARNES
Thames-side country living

Looped to the north by the Thames and home to a 120-acre green with a duck pond surrounded by trees, Barnes is all about the tranquillity from being close to the water. There are leaf-swathed streets of Victorian and Edwardian buildings – explore the cottages of Little Chelsea to the west for chocolate-box loveliness. The extraordinary expanse of the London Wetland Centre (see page 59) is also on hand for bracing, nature-filled walks. Village life clusters around Barnes High Street and is made complete with a selection of cutesy interior shops and tempting pubs that include the Sun Inn (see page 106), the White Hart (see page 103) overlooking the Thames and the Bull's Head, which hosts live jazz every night. It's between Zones 2 and 3, but you might as well be in the Cotswolds.

*Barnes overground*

HAM
Have a poke around this beautiful nook

One of Richmond's best-kept secrets, Ham Common feels as if a village green has been parachuted in from the country. It's tiny: just a small duck pond, a couple of pubs (the New Inn and the Hand and Flower are favourites) and a small wooded area. The Victorian houses surrounding the open space provide a picturesque backdrop to the regular cricket matches held here in summer. Bring a blanket and a hamper and come here on a sunny afternoon to watch one and laze on the grass.

Kingston overground

WILD WATER

A city founded on a river, the capital is dripping with places to get closer to water. London's Thames stretches from leafy, bucolic Richmond through the main blockbuster drag in the heart of town, out through the reclaimed docks of the East End and into the sticky creeks of Greenwich. However, look beyond the city's largest river and you'll find canals and waterways that wind behind streets and through parks, supporting communities of wildlife – and also of humans, bobbing cosily in their little barges. There are old reservoirs, no longer supplying drinking water but now home to huge populations of birds and beasts. There are even places you can swim, full of untamed weeds and muddy underfoot, quite out of keeping with the views of tower blocks and skyscrapers. Jump into the cold water, float on your back and drift back into nature.

A glorious sunset over the Serpentine, Regent's Park.

CREEKSIDE LOW TIDE WALKS
A fascinating, muddy way to explore a unique natural environment

Deptford Creek has a colourful history of fishing, shipbuilding and dockyards. The muddy waters are also home to a huge variety of wildlife, from shrimps and crabs to birds and flowers. The Creekside Discovery Centre is a wonderful place to find out more about this environment, running activities for families in the holidays. Every month a lucky few walkers (numbers are limited and you must book in advance) stride along a muddy riverbed in waders and get a duck's-eye view of the rapidly changing banks. It's a history lesson as well as a close-up look at some of the area's wildlife and an emotionally affecting, new perspective on an overlooked area.

creeksidecentre.org.uk/events/low-tide-walks/ ♀*14 Creekside, SE8 4SA* £
Walks once monthly, times dependent on tides *Greenwich DLR, Deptford DLR*
No wheelchair access for walks

REGENT'S CANAL
Nine miles of peace and tranquillity

Part of the Grand Union Canal, the Regent's Canal stretches like a green–blue vein from east to west, snaking from Little Venice through Paddington, Camden, King's Cross, the City, Haggerston and Hackney, into east London and Lee Valley Park. It sneaks behind the scenes of some of London's biggest attractions: walk, cycle or take a boat trip to see another side of London Zoo's aviary, watch the human zoo at Camden Market, or duck through tunnels and under bridges next to old Victorian warehouses. Observe a quieter way of life, with the bright barges and houseboats along the banks, including the bookshop barge The Word on the Water.

canalrivertrust.org.uk/enjoy-the-waterways/canal-and-river-network/regents-canal **FREE** There is wheelchair access

BOW CREEK ECOLOGY PARK
Spot birds and beasts as trains glide overhead

Uncover water-dwelling wildlife in this little haven transformed from an old ironworks. It's situated on a bend in the River Lea, just to the east of the Blackwall Tunnel Northern Approach, with views of the flying saucer-like O2 arena. Come here to escape the grind and do some twitching: there are sand martin and kingfisher boxes installed, redshanks on the mudflats and kestrels swooping down to pick off mice. The only thing that will remind you of the relentlessness of the city is the DLR, which whooshes overhead.

visitleevalley.org.uk/en/content/cms/nature/nature-reserve/bow-creek Bidder Street, E16 4ST **FREE** 8.30 a.m.–varies according to season Canning Town There is wheelchair access

HAMMERTON'S FERRY
A bucolic way to cross the river

The beautifully green area around Ham House and Eel Pie Island in Twickenham is rather lacking in the bridge-across-the-Thames department. Make the trip on the water instead. This father-and-son-operated ferry chugs back and forth across the river all day, taking passengers and bikes between the two banks. Hop on board and take a mini boat trip with stunning views of the huge houses up high on the banks of Richmond and downriver towards Eel Pie Island. There's no scheduled service – wave or holler from the bankside if the boat is on the other side of the river.

hammertonsferry.com/ ♀*Orleans Road, TW1 3BL* £ *1 March–31 October weekdays 10 a.m.–6 p.m., weekends 10 a.m.–6.30 p.m.; 1 November–30 April weekends only, weather permitting.* *St Margarets overground* *No wheelchair access*

THE ORNAMENTAL CANAL
The East End's back garden

A slick of green in a canyon of new-build flats and eighties redevelopment, Wapping's Ornamental Canal is a bolthole for East Enders and office workers. It's no longer navigable, but is a sliver of nature-friendly water that makes for a pretty place to walk or cycle. Running from the Shadwell Basin through Shadwell woods and past Tobacco Dock, it's been recently cleaned and bird boxes and platforms added: you might spot herons, ducks, carp and geese.

towerhamlets.gov.uk **FREE** *Wapping overground* *There is wheelchair access*

THE SERPENTINE
Wild swimming in the West End

Commuting to and from work in hot weather is tiring, sticky and grimy. A quiet plunge into the cool waters of the Serpentine River in Hyde Park at lunchtime will revive and invigorate, firing you up for a productive afternoon. The Lido has a large, concreted sun terrace and grassy sunbathing area, but we're all about getting away from the crazy crowds and into the unchlorinated water. Float on your back, looking up at the clouds and let the hubbub of London drift away for a few minutes. Join the Serpentine Swimming Club for daily early-morning swims.

royalparks.org.uk/parks/hyde-park/sport-in-hyde-park/serpentine-lido ♥ Hyde Park, W2 3XA £
June–August 10 a.m.–6 p.m., in May weekends and Bank Holidays only 🚌 Knightsbridge, Lancaster Gate
♿ There is wheelchair access

SHADWELL BASIN
Make like you're beside the sea at this luxurious stretch of water

Shadwell Basin is the biggest body of water in the old London Docks area. Although it's surrounded by flats and houses, it feels open, sunny and almost like a coastal harbour. Fishermen sit in tents on the scraps of green land that jut into the water, while sailors and kayakers plough through the small swell. It's a good place to visit on a summer's day, as there's often a breeze skipping off the waves and it feels like relief from the relentlessly built-up East End. However, every so often the views of Canary Wharf remind you that you're very much in the heart of the city.

shadwell-basin.co.uk ♀Glamis Road, E1W 3TD **FREE** ⏱24 hours 🚇Wapping overground ♿There is wheelchair access

WELSH HARP RESERVOIR
A wild alternative to manicured parks

This 420-acre nature reserve is a moody blur of water, marshes, trees and grasslands, perfect for long, gloomy walks in autumn, or picnics in summer. Muntjac deer skulk in the undergrowth, water voles scuttle along the banks, while ducks and grebes breed and swim among the bullrushes. It's a good place to spot rarer birds too; come in the early morning to avoid the visitors who flock here on warm days and head to the bird hides on the east bank of the water. There are also several sailing clubs based on the reservoir – try a windsurfing or sailing taster session at the Welsh Harp Sailing Club on a Thursday evening during summer for only £10.

brent.gov.uk/services-for-residents/sport-leisure-and-parks/parks/park-finder/welsh-harp-reservoir/
📍 *Birchen Grove, NW9 8SA* **FREE** ⏱ *24 hours*
🚇 *Wembley Park, Neasden* ♿ *Accessible*

BATHING PONDS ON HAMPSTEAD HEATH
Splash around with ducks and geese

Nothing wakes you up faster than a swim in chilly water, and the ponds on Hampstead Heath seem colder and wilder than most in London. In the winter they invigorate; in summer they suit more languorous strokes. There are two single-sex ponds and one mixed. The single-sex areas have a gloriously old-fashioned, bucolic feel and regulars are fiercely protective of their beloved pools. Spend all day here; bring a packed lunch and sunbathe in the meadows.

cityoflondon.gov.uk/things-to-do/green-spaces/hampstead-heath/swimming/Pages/default.aspx
📍 *Hampstead Heath, NW5 1QR* £ ⏱ *Ladies' and men's ponds opening times vary during the year. Mixed bathing ponds 7 a.m.–7 p.m.* 🚇 *Tufnell Park, Belsize Park, Archway* ♿ *There is wheelchair access*

WALKS

London's self-guided walks are perhaps one of the easiest ways to start exploring the city's greener side. They wind through the city's parks, woodlands and nature reserves, snake beside rivers and canals and worm through patches of green even in the very heart of the built-up conurbation. They're the 'greatest hits' of some of the city's most breathtaking sights and views: enjoy peeks at stately homes, pass over viaducts with far-reaching vistas, or ramble through nature-packed reserves.

Some of these routes may seem intimidatingly long, but all are broken up into manageable chunks. Cherry-pick sections and spread your walks through the seasons, stopping off at pubs for pit stops, or indulge yourself and binge-walk at weekends or holidays. We've not included wheelchair access information for these walks here, as accessibility depends so much on weather, type of wheelchair and varies even within the walks themselves.

Take in some surprising historical sights on the London LOOP.

CAPITAL RING
A sole-stirring expedition

The definitive green London walk, the Capital Ring is a 126 km trek through stunning scenery and nature reserves, under and over the Thames and via sites of scientific interest. You'll get new perspectives on familiar parts of London: the buildings and manicured playing fields of Harrow School, the Olympic Park and the dinosaurs of Crystal Palace, and see places and views you had no idea existed: the Stoke Newington reservoirs, crossing lock gates at Gallions Reach and so, so many parks. The route is divided into fifteen manageable walks, all marked by signs — some stretches take you down peaceful paths for miles. It takes in the modern — through the Olympic Park and past City airport — and the historic — from Henry VIII's childhood home Eltham Palace in the south-east, to Wharncliffe viaduct in the north-east.

tfl.gov.uk/modes/walking/capital-ring

LONDON OUTER ORBITAL PATH (LOOP)
Roam the liminal spaces where country meets city

A gigantic, 149-mile (240 km) circle around the city, rather like a green M25, the London Loop starts at Erith and meanders through the parks, farms, downs and green areas of outer London. It's studded with names you'll know from the far reaches of tube lines – Cockfosters, Upminster, Hatton Cross – and unexpected, glorious flashes of proper country seeping into the city. Explore the ancient chalk lands of Farthing Common, with its Saxon burial mounds and Neolithic tracks; Black Jack's Lock and Mill on the Grand Union Canal; or the stunning avenue of giant redwood trees at Havering Country Park. Well signposted, it's a fruitful, organized way to explore the green side of London; every one of its twenty-four manageable sections has something special and unexpected to offer.

tfl.gov.uk/modes/walking/loop-walk

PARKLAND WALK
Soar high above north London

A walk along London's longest nature reserve (four miles or six kilometres), which trails along the old railway track from Finsbury Park to Muswell Hill, taking in the highs and lows of north London. Start at Finsbury Park and wind your way along the tree-hung path, behind rows of houses, under tunnels and past abandoned railway station platforms. The walk is split into two parts; walk through Queen's and Highgate woods for the most pleasant link between them. Savour the life-sized spriggan sculpture who perches malevolently on a railway arch and the stunning views across London from the viaduct that passes over St James' Lane in Muswell Hill.

haringey.gov.uk/libraries-sport-and-leisure/parks-and-open-spaces/z-parks-and-open-spaces/parkland-walk-local-nature-reserve

THE WANDLE TRAIL
A kid-friendly trek packed with fun

This walking and cycle route tracks the River Wandle through twelve miles (19 km) of parks, gardens and green spaces, starting at East Croydon Station and snaking up to the Thames at Wandsworth (or, of course, the other way round). For the most part it's a gentle, easy stroll, with plenty to see on the way – perfect for doing in sections with kids or those who get tired. Make generous pit stops at Deen City Farm, Morden Hall Park and Wandle Meadow Nature Park for exploring, fun and ice creams. Look out for the Wandle Art Trail installations which include blue plaques, ceramic signs that commemorate passing events, such as falling in the river, that have happened to families on this route and viewing platforms that jut over the river.

sustrans.org.uk/ncn/map/route/wandle-trail

THAMES PATH
Go with the flow

The Thames Path runs along the banks of the river
for 184 miles (296 km), from the source of the river
in Kemble, Gloucestershire, to the Thames Barrier in
Woolwich. On the outskirts of the city you'll pass
Windsor Castle, Hampton Court and Kew Palace,
where the banks are predominantly green and rural-
feeling. Nearer town, the walk is a spectacular way to
see how the country flows into the city: Twickenham
and Richmond are thick with foliage and huge,
country-style houses, but as you pass through Barnes
and Putney, the river becomes busier, the towpaths
more concrete and the buildings higher. Walk the route
in easy-to-manage sections; the south bank side of the
Teddington to Putney stretch is particularly lovely.

nationaltrail.co.uk/thames-path

THE GREEN CHAIN
An emerald garland across south-east London

Taking in some of south London's most verdant areas and breathtaking sights, the Green Chain is a fifty-mile (80 km) walk, split into eleven manageable sections. Stretching from the banks of the Thames at Erith, with views across the muddy Rainham Marshes, the walk passes the gothic pile of Severndroog Castle (see page 34), the fishing boats at Southmere, Crystal Palace Park's life-size Victorian dinosaurs, the Thames Barrier and green areas including Plumstead Common and Oxleas Wood. Cleverly tracking the beautiful wild spaces that lurk behind some of the most concreted areas in the city, the walk ends up in either Dulwich Park or Nunhead Cemetery (see page 50), with its views across to the City.

tfl.gov.uk/modes/walking/green-chain-walk

EVENTS

London's rural-feeling events calendar is as jam-packed as a WI sponge cake, from the hilarious, boozy Goat Race that starts spring with a bleat, to the bountiful, pagan-feeling October Plenty held at Bankside in October and the winter-defeating twinkling lights of Syon Park's Enchanted Wonderland, brightening the darkest afternoons.

There are days to celebrate the annual reappearance of flowers that herald the warmer weather, fetes that feel as if they're taking place on a village green in the depths of the country and chances to peek behind the doors of some of our secret green patches in the heart of the city.

These events are a way to reconnect with our heritage and our agricultural present, to meet people on the same wavelength and, most importantly, to have a great day out. Mark them in your diary and enjoy.

The Berry Man bedecked with wild fruits and foliage at October Plenty.

OXFORD VS CAMBRIDGE GOAT RACE
Pun fun with four-legged competitors

Taking place on the same day as its water-based namesake, the annual Goat Race at Spitalfields City Farm is at least as much fun. Two goats, one dressed in Oxford blue, one in the lighter Cambridge blue, career around the farm cheered on by a capacity crowd (the event usually sells out way in advance). You can even make a bet on your favourite. There's enough else going on – live music, goat-e-oke, a pigs-in-tutus run – to turn this into a big day out, with proceeds raised enough to feed the farm for a whole year.

thegoatrace.org; spitalfieldscityfarm.org ♀*Buxton Street, E1 5AR* £ 🚇*Whitechapel* ♿*There is wheelchair access*

BLUEBELLS
Welcome the spring

The reappearance of bluebells unfurling and nodding gently each spring is one of the year's most heartwarming sights. They'll be at their peak towards the end of April and the beginning of May. Take the opportunity to explore some woods, snap a few pictures and rediscover the joys of a wander in the sun. Our favourite spots to find them include Holland Park, the top left-hand corner of Kew Gardens (page 21) in the woodland behind Queen's Charlotte's Cottage, Oxleas Wood and Osterley Park (page 31), where there are sometimes guided bluebell walks.

JACK-IN-THE-GREEN
A glimpse into England's pagan past

A centuries-old (or even older) tradition, Jack-in-the-Green is a flower-and-leaf-bedecked figure who is paraded around to welcome back the sun after the long winter. Every 1 May, the Deptford Jack – accompanied by musicians, a troupe wearing clown costumes and old-fashioned outfits, plus a large crowd – is marched through the streets of the borough (or sometimes through the City). Morris dancers perform at various pubs along the route and much beer is drunk. It's a wild-feeling event and a real taste of pagan England, marking the new season in a truly unique way.

🖊deptford-jack.org.uk/ 🕐 1 May, from noon **FREE** 🚇 Deptford overground, Deptford Bridge ♿ Accessible

CANALWAY CAVALCADE
Party with the boat people

Every May bank holiday, the people who live, work and play on the Regent's Canal celebrate their watery environs. There are narrowboats of all shapes and sizes to look at, Punch and Judy shows, real ale, tasty food, morris dancing and children's puppet shows on the Puppet Theatre Barge. The highlight is the parade of illuminated boats on the Sunday night.

🖊waterways.org.uk/events_festivals/canalway_ cavalcade/iwa_canalway_cavalcade 📍Warwick Crescent, W2 6NE **FREE** 🕐May Day Bank Holiday 🚇Warwick Avenue ♿Some boats have limited wheelchair access

OPEN GARDEN SQUARES
Unlock the wonders of London's secret, verdant places

For one magical weekend in June, many of the locked, walled and fenced gardens of the city are open to curious visitors. There are, of course, the private spaces such as Eaton Square, with its sharp lawns and formal beds, and the grand landscape studded with fine sculpture of Belgrave Square Gardens. However, there's also the chance to see other, less obvious, secret spaces: the Islamic-inspired Ismaili Centre roof garden, the Beech Garden in the Barbican estate and the roof garden on the tenth floor of the Blue Fin building. It's also an opportunity to peek at what the city's community gardens have in store for the year; there are housing association plots, allotments and social enterprise market gardens ripe for exploration too.

opensquares.org/ **£** One weekend in June
Limited access to some gardens

MARYLEBONE SUMMER FAYRE
The fashionista's fete

Marylebone's annual June fayre gives a decidedly chic gloss to the traditional village fete. You'll find country attractions galore – a farmers' market, farm animals to pet and craft stalls – and also cutting-edge music, bike-powered smoothie makers and special events hosted by some of the area's most glamorous stores. It's the Cath Kidston end of rurality – the chain even has a branch here – so wear your finest flower-sprigged shirt and a jaunty Panama hat and you'll feel at home.

marylebonesummerfayre.com Across Marylebone
FREE Mid-June Baker Street There is wheelchair access

LENNY
Lincoln Longwool

LAMBETH COUNTRY SHOW
Country sweetness with a hefty helping of urban grit

Our favourite country-in-the-city event, Lambeth Country Show fuses multicultural London arts with rural traditions. Stages scattered across Brockwell Park host jazz, hip-hop and reggae artists, while birds of prey soar overhead, farmers show off their prize pigs and sheep are herded through gates. Beekeeping stalls, mini zoos and farms butt up against riot-themed art projects, while samba bands perform next to morris dancers. It's a glorious, higgledy-piggledy mix of cultures that makes you grin from ear to ear – real London. Whatever you do, don't miss the always-hilarious vegetable character competition.

🖱 *lambethcountryshow.co.uk* 📍*Norwood Rd, SE24 9BJ*
FREE *Donations greatly appreciated* ⏱*Weekend in mid-July* 🚇*Herne Hill overground* ♿*There is wheelchair access*

THE FAIR IN THE SQUARE
Watch ewes jig in Highgate

Appropriately for an area so leafy and quiet, Highgate's Fair in the Square gives Londoners a taste of country life. Climb Highgate Hill for sheep-shearing (and even sheep-dancing!) displays, baking competitions, heaps of delicious food, Punch and Judy shows, circus skills workshops led by the wonderful team at nearby Jacksons Lane arts centre, a land train and bales of live music and dancing. You're only a stone's throw away from Parliament Hill if you fancy a quick ramble afterwards.

🖱 *fairinthesquare.co.uk* 📍*Highgate Square, N6 6BP*
FREE ⏱*Third Saturday in June, 12.30 p.m.–5.30 p.m.*
🚇*Highgate, Archway* ♿*There is wheelchair access*

CARTERS STEAM FAIR
Scream if you want to go faster

The reds, golds and yellows of Carters travelling funfair herald its arrival in a London park better than any flyer could. The retro stylings of its vintage steam-powered carousels, swing boats, wagons and coconut shies are more works of art than rides and stalls. The smell of candyfloss and hot coal and the sounds of laughter and screams of delight fill the air. The fair travels around London and the south-east – come on one of their firework nights for the most beautiful experience.

cartersteamfair.co.uk ♀*Various locations* £
☺*Spring until autumn* ♿*Many rides are accessible*

CULTIVATE FESTIVAL
Way to grow!

Whether you've got a window box, a garden or a smallholding, if you're green-fingered you'll love Cultivate. The Waltham Forest festival is aimed at those who grow food, with practical help such as compost giveaways, workshops and networking afternoons mixed in with fun events including street theatre, produce shows and kids activities. It's a great way to meet like-minded people, form alliances and swap clever gardening tips.

cultivatewf.org ♀*Across Waltham Forest* **FREE**
☺*September* ♿*Most venues are accessible*

OCTOBER PLENTY
A pagan-feeling celebration of harvest home

A psychedelic mix of autumn, harvest and Shakespeare, the Lions Part theatre company's October Plenty feels like a trip back hundreds, if not thousands, of years into a dark, rural past. The Corn Queene – a huge effigy fashioned from vegetables, wheat, barley and green leaves taken from Borough Market – is led by the Berry Man – the autumn incarnation of a Green Man – from the Globe Theatre to Borough Market. Once there, the company perform a play – always lustily acted and with eye-popping costumes – plus there's storytelling, apple-bobbing, morris dancing and a lot of cider and beer drinking. It's one of London's most enjoyable rural events, great for all ages and with a sense of connection to a half-forgotten, witchy past. Go.

⌕ *thelionspart.co.uk/octoberplenty* ♥ *21 New Globe Walk, Bankside, SE1 9DT* **FREE** ⏱ *Sunday in late October* 🚇*London Bridge* ♿*There is wheelchair access*

ENCHANTED WOODLAND
Brighten up your winter

Every year, the lush woodland at Syon Park in Brentford is bathed in lights, as the park is transformed into the shining Enchanted Woodland. Glasshouses become pulsing, glowing bulbs, trees twinkle with fairy lights and lasers pierce the cold night air. Warm up with a winter barbecue, mulled wine and mince pies. It's a wonderful, non-denominational way to start to feel festive. Wrap up, wear your wellies and lose yourself in wonder.

⌕ *enchantedwoodland.com* ♥ *Park Rd, TW7 6AZ* £ ⏱ *From mid-November to early December, Friday, Saturday, Sunday only, 5 p.m.–9 p.m. (last entry 8 p.m.)* 🚇*Syon Lane overground* ♿*There is wheelchair access*

PICTURE CREDITS

With a special thank you to Jeff Pitcher, for his hard work and beautiful photos (pitcherphotography.org).

Shops and Markets Pages 76–77 © Jeff Pitcher; page 78 ©ElenaChaykinaPhotography/Shutterstock.com; page 79 (left) © Chegworth Valley; page 79 (right) © Jeff Pitcher; page 80 (left) © Jeff Pitcher; page 80 (right) © Meat Butcher and Delicatessen; page 81 (left) © London Farmers' Markets; page 81 (right) © Horniman Museum and Gardens; page 82 (left) © iStock.com/IR_Stone; page 82 (right) © London Farmers' Markets; page 83 © Jeff Pitcher

The Good Life Pages 84–85 © Wildes Cheese; page 86 (left) © Rupert Fowler, courtesy of Hen Corner; page 86 (right) © Parkside Farm; page 87 (left) © Handweavers; page 87 © Organiclea; page 88 © The Green Wood Guild; page 89 (left) © Wildes Cheese; page 89 (right) © John Rensten; page 90 © Karen Liebreich, Abundance London; page 91 © Richard Reynolds/GuerrillaGardening.org

Sports and Activities Pages 92–93 © Active360.co.uk; page 94 (left) © iStock.com/stevenallan; page 94 (right) © Pavel1964/Shutterstock.com; page 95 © The Conservation Volunteers; page 96 © Active360.co.uk; page 97 (left) © Hyde Park Stables; page 97 (right) © Jeff Pitcher; page 98 (left) © iStock.com/ AnnSteer; page 98 (right) © Rogan Macdonald/Alamy; page 99 © Roswitha Chesher/Cecil Sharp House

Pubs Pages 100–101 © Young and Co.'s Brewery; page 102 (left) © Pres Panayotov/Shutterstock.com; page 102 (right) © Young and Co.'s Brewery; page 103 (left) © Jeff Pitcher; page 103 (right) © Jeff Pitcher; page 104 (left) © Dumitru Brinzan; page 104 (right) © The Orange Tree, Totteridge; page 105 © Young and Co.'s Brewery; page 106 © Jeff Pitcher; page 107 (left) © Jeff Pitcher; page 107 (right) © Young and Co.'s Brewery

Villages Pages 108–109 © Young and Co.'s Brewery; page 110 (top) © iStock.com/Memitina; page 110 (bottom) © iStock.com/oversnap; page 111 (left) © Jeff Pitcher; page 111 (right) © 4kclips/Shutterstock.com; page 112 (left) © Dunn's Bakery; page 112 (right) © Jeff Pitcher; page 113 (top) © Piero Cruciatti/Alamy; page 113 (bottom) © Michael Heath/Alamy; page 114 © Loop Images/Getty Images; page 115 © Jeff Pitcher

Wild Water Pages 116–117 © Jeff Pitcher; page 118 © Jeff Pitcher; page 119 (left) © Jeff Pitcher; page 119 (right): photo courtesy of Lee Valley Regional Park Authority; page 120 © Jeff Pitcher; page 121 © Jeff Pitcher; page 122 © Jeff Pitcher; page 123 (left) © Andrew Self; page 123 (right) © John Farnham/Alamy

Walks Pages 124–125 © Jeff Pitcher; page 126 (top left) © Judith Palmer; page 126 (top right) © Nando Machado/Shutterstock.com; page 126 (bottom right) © Ron Ellis/Shutterstock.com; page 127 © Jeff Pitcher; page 128 © Sylvie Jarrossay/Alamy; page 129 © Jeff Pitcher; page 130 © Jeff Pitcher; page 131 © Jeff Pitcher

Events Pages 132–133 © Jeff Pitcher; page 134 (left) © London News Pictures/REX/Shutterstock; page 134 (right) © iStock.com/AnnSteer; page 135 (left) © Sarah Crofts; page 135 (right) © The Inland Waterways Association; page 136 (left) Diana Jarvis, courtesy of Open Garden Squares; page 136 (right) © The Howard de Walden Estate; page 137 (left): courtesy of The Fair in the Square; page 137 (right) © Georgia Merton, courtesy of Lambeth Country Show; page 138 (left) © mubus7/Shutterstock.com; page 138 (right), courtesy of Cultivate Festival; page 139 (left) © Jeff Pitcher; page 139 (right) © Simon Hadleigh-Sparks

ACKNOWLEDGEMENTS

This book is for:

Jeff Pitcher, who gets it so completely; Arthur and Dusty Jenkinson – the sparkiest and funniest of children; and Rhona and Colin Hodges, for their constant support and patience.

Grateful thanks to:

Katy Parker at Michael O'Mara Books for her help, enthusiasm and steady hand; Juliet Pickering for her agent superpowers; Rhona Hodges for child-wrangling and word-checking; Charlie Mounter for her sensitive and insightful copy-editing; Darren Jordan, Claire Cater and Judith Palmer for their hard work; and to all the people and organizations who kindly let us use their pictures.

Huge appreciation to everyone who helped me find the green:

Tom Hodges, Gareth Jenkinson, Sarra Manning, Mark Bolton, Andie McGrath, Natasha Morabito, Samantha Veal, Charley Stone, Delia Sparrow, Baron Schwartz, Paul McLoone, Louise Taft, Atalanta Kernick, Edward Rekkers, Carrie Stewart, Michelle Kerr, Amanda May, Cassandra Fox, Jennifer Carey, Robert Flood, Sharon O'Dea, Val Gwyther, Shelley Ward, Nicola Key, Pandora Vaughan, Emma Chesters, Jim Bishop, Juliet Kinsman, Roz Kerr, Sophie Davies, Keiko Shimmer-Muller, Katherine Burkinshaw, Michael Buffalo Bar, Sarah Rabia, Mike Mansfield, Davina Mashru, Flora Bathurst, Arthur Scott, Lisa Berenson, Toby Manning, Brian Kotz, David Westcott, Thursday Angell.